Philosophy
of Law

Philosophy of Law
A Brief Introduction

Edmund L. Pincoffs

Professor Emeritus
University of Texas

Wadsworth Publishing Company
Belmont, California
A Division of Wadsworth, Inc.

Philosophy Editor: Kenneth King
Consulting Editor: James Sterba
Editorial Assistant: Cynthia Campbell
Production: Mary Douglas
Print Buyer: Martha Branch
Designer: John Osborne
Copy Editor: Betty Duncan-Todd
Compositor: TBH Typecast, Inc.
Cover: Al Burkhardt

Printed in the United States of America

1 2 3 4 5 6 7 8 9 10—95 94 93 92 91

Library of Congress Cataloging-in-Publication Data

Pincoffs, Edmund L.
    Philosophy of law : a brief introduction / Edmund L. Pincoffs.
        p.   cm.
    Includes index.
    ISBN 0-534-14802-6
    1. Criminal law—Philosophy. 2. Law—Philosophy. 3. Law and
    ethics.   I. Title.
K5018.P56   1991   90-12897
340'.1—dc20   CIP

Contents

P A R T   T W O

Responsibility 47

| P   A   R   T   T   H   R   E   E |

Law and Morality   89

Preface

This book is an introduction. It offers a way into the seemingly amorphous complex of problems, theories, and arguments that constitute the philosophy of law. It is not a textbook. It makes no pretense of "covering," or even tipping its hat to, the wide range of subjects that philosophers of law discuss. The book asks three questions in its three parts: Can legal punishment be justified? Can holding persons liable for harm be justified? What are the appropriate relations between legal and moral concerns?

The first question requires an answer to the second, and the second demands an answer to the third. My aim is to exhibit the way in which philosophical inquiry moves backstage in its attempt to understand what is happening on the forestage—how conceptual questions and fundamental questions of principle must be explored if large social issues are to be *understood,* to say nothing of resolving them. But my aim is not merely to show forth the glories of philosophy. It is to find answers, however tentative and incomplete, to my questions or at least to point a direction in which answers might be found.

Thus, there is one way in which this book hangs together—as a set of interrelated questions. Another way is in the identification of a common subject matter. Punishment, responsibility-ascription, and law can be understood as practices or as nests or families of practices. What needs justification, if particular instances of punishment, responsibility-ascription, or adjudication are to be justified, is the *practice* in accordance with which those who punish, hold liable, or decide cases make their moves. But practices have certain characteristics in common, and the standards against which they are judged may be closely related. That, anyway, is an assumption that I have found useful.

My motive in choosing the three questions discussed here is not merely to intrigue the reader, nor even to contribute to the solution of social problems. It is also to take a path into the philosophy of law that, however winding and branching, leads naturally and coherently to some of the great historical topics, including especially that of the nature of law. I hope that the reader will find this book a useful entryway into a vast subject.

Acknowledgments

This book has in its slow progress toward publication incurred a great many debts of gratitude. I should especially like to thank Richard Rodewald, John Hodson, Noah Lemos, Thomas Seung, Robert Kane, and other University of Texas colleagues for reading or listening to and discussing some part of the manuscript. The invitation to deliver the Second Romanell Lecture to the American Philosophical Association provided an opportunity to rethink the argument of Part 2 on Responsibility. My debt to Joel Feinberg in that part is deep and pervasive. My cousin, the late Maurice C. Pincoffs, Jr., read the whole of the manuscript for legal mistakes and challenged some of my conclusions with characteristic flair and verve. I owe special thanks to Wadsworth Publishing Company's manuscript reviewers: John Arthur, State University of New York, Binghampton; Gerald Dworkin, University of Illinois at Chicago; Richard Haynes, University of Florida, Gainesville; Donald C. Hubin, The Ohio State University; Ronald Moore, University of Washington; Beth Nolan, George Washington University; and William Starr, Marquette University. I hope that they will think the changes I have made to meet their criticisms have improved the book. I am most grateful to Mary Douglas for the care with which she has managed the production of my manuscript.

I should like to thank Oxford University Press for permission to quote from Patrick Devlin, *Enforcement of Morals,* 1965; Stevens and Sons for permission to quote from Alf Ross, *On Law and Justice,* 1958; and Harvard University Press for permission to quote from Ronald Dworkin, *Law's Empire,* 1986.

As always, my greatest debt is to Mary Elizabeth Pincoffs for quiet support and amazing patience.

Castine, Maine
July, 1990

Introduction

Think of the philosophy of law as a grand and rambling old mansion with recently added wings and outbuildings. Each room contains a new topic, a separate subject. There are two ways to approach such a structure — two conceptions of what one is doing in exploring it. One way is to attempt to draw up as detailed a sketch as possible, given one's limitations of time and energy. Ideally, each room will be accounted for, and the contents inventoried. This, one might think, is a necessary preliminary to understanding the whole structure in relation to its parts. The other way is to find an intriguing entrance and to explore just those passageways and spaces that seem to lead from one to another, beckoning the investigator beyond the ground floor rooms to the attic, the basement, the new wings, the outbuildings, and the neighborhood. The first approach is systematic and comprehensive, the second may seem intuitive and impressionistic. Much can be said for either approach, but in a brief introduction such as this, the latter seems more appropriate.

The line of problems I discuss in this book tracks the development of my own interest in the philosophy of law. That interest began when I discovered, to my astonishment, that there was no generally agreed-on theory to explain why a government may do terrible things to people who violate its laws: hang them, transport them to foreign lands, consign them to hard labor, or confine them to prison cells. Worse, I discovered that the two main theories offered to justify these terrible things, retributivism and utilitarianism, were inconsistent; both could not be accepted logically. I wrote a book on that subject to try to reconcile the theories. That project led me to recognize that, underlying the problem of justifying the practice of punishment, there lay the deeper problem of how, on what grounds, to justify the pervasive practice of holding people responsible for their misdeeds, including their violations of law. At that point, I realized that there is the further problem of how to set off legal from moral responsibility and, more generally, how to distinguish legal from moral issues. This is the order that I follow here: punishment, responsibility, and the relation of law to morality. I hope that you will find them as intriguing as I do.

The boundaries of the philosophy of law are hard to make precise because they are determined by the different interests of people who are reflective about law and, in reflection, are led to wonder about the meaning, relations, and cultural context of the family of concepts or ideas, of which law is but one. But that is not the whole story. Why should philosophers or anyone else worry about the meaning of such concepts as punishment, responsibility, law, morality, rule, right, justice, or happiness? Very often, it is because people believe that establishing the meaning of such notions is a necessary preliminary to justifying choices or decisions concerning policies or practices in which they play a central role.

For example, some believe that, before we can turn to the question whether a given policy is a just one, we must ferret out the meaning of justice and the criteria of its application to particular cases. Whether this order of business can always, or ever, be followed is a complex matter. Even though we may want to follow it, difficulties arise in doing so. If we say, for example, that the meaning of justice is that those and only those policies that are conducive to the happiness of everyone are just, then we have already adopted a position about which policies are just. We have attempted to define our way out of a substantive problem about competing standards of justice, a problem that cannot be resolved by stipulating this or that definition. Or if we say that the meaning of justice is that relevantly like cases should be treated alike and relevantly different cases treated differently, we do have a formal and neutral formula. This formula, however, has no application until a substantive question is answered: What counts as a relevant likeness or difference?

Definitional questions may be difficult to keep distinct from substantive ones, but it is important to try to keep them distinct. For example, I agree with those philosophers who insist on a distinction between the questions of what is to count as a law and of what is to count as a good law. Keeping such matters distinct is, however difficult, an elementary necessity in the philosophical analysis of law or of any other region of philosophical concern.

PRACTICES

In this book, I often make use of the notion of a practice. I describe legal punishment, the ascription of personal responsibility, and law itself as practices. By a *practice*, I mean a rule-governed activity that specifies roles and what must, may, or may not be done by or to the players of those roles. Standing in line to buy a ticket or to check out groceries is a practice. Woe be unto the person who does not understand the rule that as Last-Comer he does not have the same rights as First-Comer and therefore does not take the end-of-the-line position!

The motivating concern of the questions I discuss is which range of practices is preferable, which practices should be instituted, changed, or abandoned. As we trace out practices and the arguments for and against them, we find that to understand one practice we may first have to understand another within which it is nested, which underlies it, or with which it is to be contrasted. Thus, an investigation of the rational foundations of the practice of legal punishment leads to questions about alternative practices for the discouragement of crime, about the allied practices of holding people responsible for harm, and about the family of practices that constitute government by law. As we will see, law consists, roughly speaking, in the overall practice of publicly proclaiming and enforcing a set of rules, and it involves procedures for determining whether, and how seriously, the rules have been violated. As we think about the practice of law, a whole set of questions arises about the need for or desirability of providing a means by which we can make agreements and specify common understandings that enhance our ability to plan our lives.

RULES AND ROLES

Because I have defined practices by use of "rules" and "roles," a few words about these notions may be helpful. If I am playing baseball, my actions are governed by the rules of the game, and my role can be specified in terms of those rules. The rules prescribe that the batter is limited to three strikes and provide for no exceptions. I am the batter; I have had three strikes; I cannot earn a longer time at bat; I am out. Whoever does not understand this does not yet understand the game of baseball. Games are a kind (or a set of kinds) of practice; but the rules and roles of practices like punishment or responsibility–ascription can be less clear and more controverted and complex than those of games.

Practice rules are not to be confused with habits, patterns of behavior, what people do "as a rule," or what people "make it a rule" to do. I may make it a rule to tap home plate with my bat, and as a rule I may do it because tapping has become a habit or a pattern of my behavior. But in tapping home plate as I come to bat, I am not obeying a rule in the sense in which I do obey one when I leave the plate, instead of running to first, after striking out. To speak of a habit or a pattern of action is to speak of what a given individual, or set of individuals, tends to do under certain circumstances. To speak of a rule of a practice is to speak of what the player of a given role is required to do under the practice. The prediction that a given player, or the members of a given team, will tap home plate is based on past evidence; the prediction that batters will relinquish their turn at bat after three strikes is based on the rules of the practice of baseball.

Philosphers sometimes speak of the internal and external aspects of rules with this distinction in mind. Rules from the internal point of view are obeyed and followed and govern action. Given the practice in which I am engaged, they establish what I am required to do and lay out my rights, duties, and the standards to which I should adhere. I can appeal to them in justifying the actions I take. It is sufficient justification of my turning away from home plate that I have had three strikes. From the external point of view of a person uninformed about the rules of the practice of baseball, patterns of players turning away after three strikes and of tapping home plate are simply so many observed regularities. When I speak of a practice as a complex of rules and roles, I have in mind rules from the internal point of view.[1]

A SKETCH OF THE BOOK

Chapters 1 and 2 open the philosophical debate about punishment, the practice of legal punishment. These chapters raise the question of how punishment is to be defined and examine the utilitarian and retributive theories that claim to justify punishment. We discover the impasse resulting from the mutual inconsistency and equal plausibility of those theories and seek a way of going on from there. We notice the weaknesses of each theory and explore ways to salvage what is defensible in them. Given more guarded versions of utilitarianism and retributivism, Chapter 3 seeks a wider perspective on the whole question of the justification of punishment. We note the possibility that when the weaknesses in the theories are shored up they may find a fit with one another. We find the problem of justifying punishment still to be a very difficult one. We approach the problem by considering legal punishment as one among a number of possible practices for dealing with the inevitable tendency of some people to violate rules. Considered in this light, punishment may be complementary to other practices and is not easily eliminable, on practical or moral grounds, from the range of ways in which crime might be reduced.

Part Two turns to a larger question that may have troubled the reader throughout the discussion of punishment: How can anyone be punished justifiably for a crime if she could not help committing it? This leads to an analysis of the very practice of ascribing responsibility. Chapter 4 looks at some of the varieties of skepticism concerning the ascription of responsibility: scientific, metaphysical, practical, technological, moral, and religious. We then notice some of the trends toward reduced responsibility that flow from one or another of these skeptical perspectives.

Chapter 5 takes a close look at the practices of responsibility–ascription. (It turns out that there is a family of practices rather than just one.) It surveys the nature and varieties of personal responsibility and examines the concepts of *harm* and *act* that inevitably arise in such a survey. This survey highlights the importance of the various categories of defense that can be offered by a person who is prima facie liable for the harm he may have brought about. Thus, Chapter 6 looks at the insanity defense and asks why there should be any defenses at all. Chapter 7 then confronts the skeptical question of whether, and if so why, responsibility–ascription deserves to survive. The suggested approach involves comparing responsibility–ascription to other practices for the spreading of losses across a population. The chapter suggests a way around obstacles thrown up by skeptics concerning individual responsibility.

Part Three concerns itself with more general questions about the relations of law and morality than those that involve responsibility. Chapter 8 sketches and criticizes the three traditional theories of the nature of law: legal positivism, legal realism, and natural law theory. Chapter 9 asks whether there is a conception of morality that will, along with a defensible conception of law, make possible meaningful discussion of the relations between morality and law. Here I point out some of the difficulties in thinking of morality as a domain of rules and principles, a kind of quasi-law. I suggest that this way of thinking about morality is unnecessarily constrained, that we need a broader conception that includes the morality of character—of what the ancients called the virtues and vices. Chapter 10 then picks up that suggestion as a possibly useful one in delineating the proper domains of morality and law—the idea being, roughly, that morality is primarily concerned with what kind of person to be, whereas law is fundamentally concerned with what and what not to do. The argument of the chapter revolves around the differing roles, in legal and moral judgment, of the defenses recognized in Part Two.

The last two chapters analyze what I call moral pressures on the law and legal pressures on morality. Chapter 11 considers the force of the criticism of a system of law that it is unjust, particularly in a society that professes egalitarian ideals. This leads to a more general discussion of justice as a social ideal. In the course of the discussion, four principles for the moral assessment of a legal system are set out. The problem of conscientious refusal to obey the law is mooted, as is the question of how—and within what limits—the architects of a legal system might make room for conscientious refusal. Chapter 12 takes up two related questions. The first is when, if ever, moral beliefs should be legally enforced. The focus is on the debate between Lord Devlin and H. L. A. Hart over the proposal to prohibit homosexual activity in private between consenting adults. The second is whether government is justified in mandating moral-education programs and, if so, within what limits.

The question of what, if anything, justifies imprisoning or executing people will serve then as a door through which one may enter the philosophy of law. One is soon led from that door down connecting corridors that open into the major questions discussed here. Many of those questions are conceptual, and it becomes apparent that often to grasp a concept (for example, punishment or responsibility) it is necessary to understand the practice within which the concept has its use. The companion issues have to do with how a given practice may be justified. We find then that justification involves noticing the comparative advantages and disadvantages, practical and moral, of alternative practices that may serve the same purposes. Punishment is contrasted with social pressure as a means for the reduction of crime. We compare the ascription of personal responsibility for losses to the arbitrary allocation of losses. The aim of this procedure is to find more careful answers to these difficult philosophical issues than those that are sometimes given. The question of how a practice fits among its competitors discourages all-or-none answers.

By contrast with Parts One and Two, where the question is whether a practice can be justified and, if so, how to justify it, Part Three concerns itself with what properly falls within a practice—the practice of law. To what extent should moral beliefs and principles be encoded in law? That there should be law as a practice is not questioned, as we *do* question whether and within what limits there should be legal punishment or the ascription of responsibility.

In each of the three parts, I take a position: for legal punishment and responsibility–ascription, against the criminalization of morality, but for required moral education. My excuse is that I have been unable to resist entering the debate. My justification is that in doing so I hope to stimulate you to enter too, to criticize my proposed answers, and to offer your resolution of the daunting problems we now face.

| NOTES

1. For further discussion of the internal and external aspects of rules, see Hart, 1961, pp. 55–60, and 1983, pp. 13–15.

Punishment

C H A P T E R   1

The Problem of Punishment

HOW THE PROBLEM ARISES

The subject of this chapter is legal punishment. It should not be confused with any other sort of punishment, for example, the punishment of children or the "punishment" an investor takes in a declining stock market. For the time being, let's say that legal punishment is giving unwanted treatment to persons who have violated the law. We'll try for a more precise definition later.

Why worry about the justification of legal punishment? It has been with us at least since Old Testament times. Isn't it then a waste of effort to look for its justification? We have always circulated our blood, but no one asks for our justification for doing so. We have always been attracted by gravity, but we don't bother to justify that either.

There is a difference between punishing and circulating our blood or being attracted by gravity. We can choose to continue or to abolish punishing, but the other two "activities" are not matters of choice. We don't really "do" them at all; they just happen to us. Punishing is something that we do; we are agents who engage in that kind of activity, who play roles in the practice of punishment. A world without punishment is conceivable. Robert Owen (1771–1858) is an example of an antipunishment reformer who has imagined such a world.

Owen, a Scottish industrialist, believed that no one was responsible for his deeds, that people are determined to commit crime by the environment in which they are raised to adulthood. When he established a self-governed colony in Indiana, the problem of what to do about people who violate the law was for him more than theoretical. Owen thought that proper training would eliminate most

9

crimes and that a working system of arbitration would eliminate most causes of dispute. But, said Owen in his rules for New Harmony, if "through mental disease" a person should "act in opposition to the happiness of society" he is to be placed in a "house of recovery." If he still continues in his obstreperous ways, it will be necessary to "intimate to him that unless the cause of complaint be removed they are instructed to expel him from the community" (Owen, 1842, Rule 33). We can only speculate how the "house of recovery" or expulsion from the community would have been regarded by the criminal.

Whatever Owen's benign intentions, the banished malefactor must surely have regarded himself as *punished*. Owen's experience suggests that, even if some form of determinism be granted, there remains the practical difficulty of finding adequate substitute practices for punishment.

If Owen is an exemplar of those who are opposed to punishment because they believe that no one is responsible for his deeds, Leo Tolstoy exemplifies those who reject punishment because it is inconsistent with their religious beliefs. Tolstoy held that punishment cannot be reconciled with Jesus' teachings. In his essays and in his last novel, *Resurrection*, Tolstoy returns again and again to this theme. How can we live as Christians and at the same time punish people? We are just like the people that we punish. We and they are but individual persons. But as role players in the judicial process that includes punishment, we hide in our roles. Worse, the responsibility for the things that are done to criminals seems systematically elusive:

> "Yes, killed," he said, repeating to himself the words he had used to his sister. And in his imagination, in the midst of all other impressions, there arose with wonderful clearness the beautiful face of the second dead convict, with the smile on the lips, the severe expression of brows, and the small, firm ear below the shaven, bluish skull.
>
> "And what seems terrible," he thought, "is that while he has been murdered, no one knows who murdered him. Yet he has been murdered. He was led out by Maslenikov's orders like all the rest of the prisoners. Maslenikov probably gave the usual order, signing with his stupid flourish a paper with a printed heading, and most certainly did not consider himself guilty. Still less will the careful doctor who examined the convicts. He performed his duty accurately and separated the weak. How could he foresee this terrible heat, or the fact that they would start so late in the day and in such crowds? The prison inspector? But the inspector only carried into execution the order that on a given day a certain number of exiles and convicts—men and women—were to be sent off. The convoy officer cannot be guilty either, for his business was to receive a certain number of persons at a certain place

and to deliver up the same number. He conducted them in the usual manner, and could not foresee that two such strong men as those I saw would be unable to stand it, and would die. No one is guilty, and yet the men have been murdered by these people who are not guilty of their death. . . .

"If a psychological problem were set to find means of making men of our time—Christian, humane, simple, kind people—perform the most horrible crimes without feeling guilty, only one solution could be devised: simply to go on doing what is being done now. It is only necessary that these people should be governors, inspectors, policemen; that they should be fully convinced that there is a kind of business called Government Service, which allows men to treat other men as things without having brotherly relations with them; and that they should be so linked together by this Government Service that the responsibility for the results of their deeds should not fall on any one of them individually." (Tolstoy, pp. 359–363)

Fyodor Dostoyevsky seems, in his novel *Crime and Punishment*, to oppose legal punishment on the ground that the only meaningful punishment is what the criminal inflicts on himself. The novel probes the excruciatingly agonized inner life—the denials, rationalizations, inner debates, delerium, bravado, and terror—of a student, Raskolnikov, who has murdered a defenseless old woman. Mere imprisonment, or even execution, could only be a relief from such a life. Raskolnikov's surrender to the authorities and thus to the workings of the criminal law becomes a merely anticlimactic event in the novel.

These are some of the reasons, then, for opposing legal punishment: no responsibility in the criminal, religious belief, and the conviction that, compared to inner suffering, legal punishment is meaningless. But the case against punishment can be made in a morally more direct way. To punish a person is to harm him; to harm a person is prima facie morally wrong. That is to say, it is wrong unless there is some satisfactory justification or excuse for inflicting the harm. The dentist may offer an acceptable reason for painfully removing a tooth. The health department may be able to justify quarantine. What general reasons can be given for legally punishing people? As we will see, the reasons that are given conflict. But before turning to the conflict, let's be more clear about the harm of punishment, and, above all, let's try to understand more exactly what punishment is—the nature of punishment.

THE HARM OF PUNISHMENT

A survey of the ways people have been punished under law carries with it a certain morbid fascination. For the Greeks, banishment from the community was one of the more severe punishments. Or the criminal could suffer *atimia*, full or partial loss of his civil rights. For example, he could lose the right to speak in a public assembly, to enter the marketplace, or to leave Athens. The Greeks practiced capital punishment not only by stoning, and by the well-known administration of poison hemlock, but also by pushing off a cliff into a convenient chasm or by exposure to the elements (Gagarin, Chs. 5 and 6; Newman, Chs. 1–3).

In eighteenth-century England, criminals could be imprisoned, consigned to the galleys, or "transported" to Australia or Georgia. But the form of punishment most vividly before the public was hanging. There were some 200 capital offenses. People could be and regularly were hanged for burglary, robbery, larceny in dwelling houses, housebreaking, horse and cattle stealing, and forgery of currency. Hangings were public spectacles attracting crowds of people. But the spectacles were so far from succeeding in the deterrence of crime that the picking of pockets, which was also a capital offense, flourished in the shadow of the gallows (Radzinowicz, Chs. 6 and 7; Stephen, Ch. 13).

With the decline of capital punishment in most jurisdictions, despite a recent revival in the United States, the most popular punishment in the United States, Britain, and Western Europe—and in much of the rest of the world—has been imprisonment. Descriptions by prisoners of the life to which they are subjected are horrifying. They are threatened by and often left at the mercy of other prisoners. They suffer rape, wounding, and sometimes death. They are bullied and reduced to seeking the protection of subgroups within the prison population. Jack Abbott, a long-time inmate, says,

> I have been made over-sensitive—my very flesh has been made to suffer sensations and longings I never had before. I have been chopped to pieces by a life of deprivation of sensations. . . . I have had my mind turned into steel by the endless smelter of time in confinement. I have been twisted by justice the way other men can be twisted by love. (pp. 44–45)

Imprisonment means loss of freedom, isolation from family and friends, loss of livelihood, indignity, forced association with other criminals, suffering, and possible injury or death. Capital punishment (typically accompanied by years of imprisonment while the appeals of the verdict move through the courts) means the loss of life itself. Although in the end the justification for imprisonment must be differentiated from the justification, if any, for capital punishment, what is at issue now is the question of whether, and if so how, *any* kind of punishment can be shown to be morally acceptable.

WHAT PUNISHMENT IS

To turn now, however, to the question whether punishment can be justified would be to move too fast. What, exactly, *is* it that is or is not justified? Here is a definition that should be suitable for our purpose of examining contending justificatory theories. Legal punishment is a practice having the following four characteristics:

1. There is a system of threats, officially promulgated, that should given legal rules be violated, given consequences, generally regarded as undesirable, will be inflicted on the violator.

2. The threatened undesirable consequences are inflicted only upon persons found guilty of violating the rules in question and only for violation of those rules.

3. The finding of guilt and imposition and administration of the undesirable consequences are by authorized agents of the system promulgating the legal rules violated.

4. The authorized agents of the system must be acting within their official capacities, not as private persons.

The threats are hypothetical ones. They are of the form: If you do so and so, then you will suffer such and such. They are not categorical—of the form: we will do such and such to you. The threats are directed toward persons specified not by name but by their description as violators of law: "breaking and entering" or "driving while intoxicated." The authority in question may, so far as the definition is concerned, be derived from appointment, descent, designation by a supernatural being, election, or any other source. It is necessary only that there be rules of the legal system in question, according to which the claim to be an authorized agent of the system can be validated.

There must be a reasonably clear indication of what is threatened. In the practice of punishment, as we will understand it, we can't threaten law violaters that something bad will happen to them, depending, say, on the zany inspiration of Gilbert and Sullivan's "Lord High Executioner"—whose "object all-sublime" is to "let the punishment fit the crime." The unpleasant consequences that are threatened must also be ones that nearly everyone wants to avoid, even though there may be masochists or guilt-ridden Raskolnikovs who want to suffer them.

Finally, the leading feature of punishment is that it intends to cause pain, suffering, loss, embarrassment, or inconvenience to the person punished. This distinguishes punishment from otherwise similar legal measures. The tax on cigarettes, for example, is not a punishment for smoking, nor is quarantine punishment for contracting typhoid.

Although this definition serves our immediate purpose, we should not think that it will resolve all issues that can arise concerning the boundaries of legal punishment. For example, in *Flemming v. Nestor* (80 S. Ct. 1367 [1960]) the Supreme Court had to decide whether the deprivation of Nestor's Social Security benefits constituted punishment. Nestor, an alien immigrant long residing in this country, had for a period been a member of the Communist party in the United States. After he had ceased to be a member, laws were enacted requiring aliens who were or had been members of the Communist party to be deported and stripped of their benefits. If the deprivation of benefits had been punishment, it would have violated several established principles of federal law, among them the principle that no one should be punished who has not been tried and that no one should be punished for doing what at the time was legal. Nestor argued that, in depriving him of his Social Security benefits, Flemming, the Secretary of Health, Education, and Welfare, was punishing him. The secretary argued that he was not punishing but merely denying a benefit and that it is within the legitimate powers of government to determine who will and will not receive benefits. The court found in favor of Flemming.

Both Nestor and Flemming could have found support for their positions in our definition. It is probably impossible to formulate a definition that will obviate future dispute about particular cases. But our definition does help focus the debate over the justification of punishment. What needs to be justified is the practice of punishment. To whatever extent features of that practice are eliminated, altered, or added, the question about justification will shift to the new subject. The best that can be claimed for the present definition is that it is wide enough to cover most of what most writers have in mind when they debate the moral acceptability of punishment.

UTILITARIANS ON PUNISHMENT

Consciously to inflict pain, loss, misery, or deprivation on a person is to do what is morally wrong unless there is some very good reason why, morally speaking, it may be done. What is that very good reason? Here we run head-on into a radical disagreement, and we discover an embarrassment for the theory of punishment. The radical disagreement is between those who hold that the only good reason for punishing is the hoped-for good consequences of doing so and those who believe that it is only what the criminal deserves that can justify punishment. The advocates of consequence are utilitarians; the proponents of desert are retributivists. The embarrassment for the theory of punishment consists in this: While these two theoretical positions are the leading candidates for a moral justification of punishment, a decision between them is very difficult, and they are inconsistent. They cannot both be true.

Let's turn first to the classic utilitarian position, the position of philosophers and legal reformers in the tradition of Jeremy Bentham (1748–1832) and William Paley (1743–1805). Their view can be summarized in the following propositions:

1. The only acceptable reason for punishing a person is that punishing her will help prevent or reduce crime.

2. The only acceptable reason for punishing a person in a given manner or degree is that this is the manner or degree most likely to reduce or prevent crime.

3. People should be punished only if punishing is the best way to prevent or reduce crime.

If you are a utilitarian judge, then you, in sentencing, look to the future. You are entirely concerned with what good punishment is likely to do for everyone concerned. Your overall aim, as a utilitarian, is to do what you can to maximize the happiness of everyone. Crime must be prevented or reduced because it is a barrier to happiness. Good consequences are consequences that maximize happiness and minimize misery. Call this the principle of utility (concern for the well-being — the happiness and absence of misery — of other human beings).[1]

Utilitarian judges and legislators consider punishment as only one of the measures for dealing with crime. The chief value of punishment consists in its deterring or preventing crime. Punishment is a general deterrent if it deters other potential criminals from crime, for fear they will suffer what the convicted criminal suffers. It is a special deterrent if it discourages the criminal herself from committing crime.

Punishment, in the nature of the case, causes some misery, the misery of the criminal. A good utilitarian has to show therefore that punishment is preferable to crime-reducing measures that cause less, or no, misery. Among other ways of preventing or reducing crime, classic (and modern) utilitarians consider means of reducing temptations to crime. Examples of such means are legislation controlling the sale of explosives or of easily concealed arms, warnings against leaving portable property unwatched or unlocked, or the printing of difficult-to-reproduce currency. In designing a criminal code, utilitarians consider such matters as motivating the criminal contemplating a crime to commit the less serious of the alternative crimes he may have in mind. For example, if the penalty for rape as well as for murder is execution, the rapist will have no incentive, so far as the criminal code is concerned, not to murder his victim.

From the utilitarian point of view, no penal legislation is warranted that is ineffective, cannot serve to prevent crime. This rules out *ex post facto laws*, laws that are not adequately promulgated, and the punishment of infants, insane persons, or persons who were physically compelled to do what they did. Penal legislation must also not be unprofitable or needless. It is unprofitable if it would produce worse consequences, with respect to the general happiness, than the offense it is meant to prevent — for example, the eighteenth-century penalty of execution for stealing bleaching goods from the bleaching grounds. It is needless if the crime can be prevented or discouraged at a lower cost in misery than punishment—for example, by early childhood instruction.

To be guided by what the criminal deserves is, from the classic utilitarian point of view, to be confused or misled. Paley puts the point clearly:

> The crime must be prevented by some means or other; and consequently whatever means appear necessary to that end, whether they be proportionable to the guilt of the criminal or not, are adopted, rightly, because they are adopted upon the principle which alone justifies the infliction of punishment at all. . . . The very end for which human government is established, requires that its regulations be adapted to the suppression of crimes. This end, whatever it may do in the plans of infinite wisdom, does not in the designation of temporal penalties, always coincide with the proportionate punishment of guilt. (Paley, Vol. II, Book VI, Ch. 9)

RETRIBUTIVISTS ON THE SAME SUBJECT

For every proposition in the classic utilitarian position, there is a classic retributivist counterproposition:

1. The only acceptable reason for punishing a person is that he has committed a crime.

2. The only acceptable reason for punishing a person in a given manner and degree is that the punishment is what he deserves.

3. Whoever commits a crime must be punished in accordance with his desert.

The retributivist judge and the retributivist jury look *back* to what the criminal has done. What counts, all that counts, in determining what she deserves is precisely what she has done, the seriousness of her crime. The possible or probable consequences of punishing the criminal are irrelevant. Immanuel Kant (1724–1804) is the great paradigm of the classic retributivist:

> Judicial punishment can never be used as a means to promote some other good for the criminal himself or for civil society, but instead it must in all cases be imposed on him only on the ground that he has committed a crime; for a human being can never be manipulated merely as a means to the purposes of someone else. . . . The law concerning pun-

ishment is a categorical imperative, and woe to him who rummages around in the winding paths of a theory of happiness looking for some advantage to be gained by releasing the criminal from punishment or by reducing the amount of it — in keeping with the Pharisaic motto: "It is better that one man should die than that the whole people should perish." If legal justice perishes, then it is no longer worth while for men to remain alive on this earth. (Kant, 1797, pp. 331–332)

When it comes to the question of how and how much the criminal is to be punished, Kant insists that nothing should be taken into account but what the criminal has done. How can a system of punishment be formulated that is strictly and solely based on the nature of the crime? Kant's answer is what he calls the principle of equality, the principle that

> . . . any undeserved evil that you inflict on someone else among the people is one that you do to yourself. If you vilify him, you vilify yourself; if you steal from him, you steal from yourself; if you kill him, you kill yourself. Only the Law of retribution (*jus talionis*) can determine exactly the kind and degree of punishment. . . . All other standards fluctuate back and forth and, because extraneous considerations are mixed with them, they cannot be compatible with the principle of pure and strict justice. (Kant, 1797, p. 332)

So far, Kant has told us how and how much we must punish *if* we punish. But he also holds that crime must meet its desert, that we have an obligation to punish crime in accordance with its desert:

> Even if a civil society were to dissolve itself by common agreement of all its members (for example, if the people inhabiting an island decided to separate and disperse themselves around the world), the last murderer remaining in prison must first be executed, so that everyone will duly receive what his actions are worth and so that the bloodguilt thereof will not be fixed on the people because they failed to insist on carrying out the punishment; for if they fail to do so, they may be regarded as accomplices in this public violation of legal justice. (Kant, 1797, p. 333)

The positions are then contraries. The conjunction of the utilitarian propositions previously listed is the contrary of the conjunction of the retributivist ones. Classic retributivism and classic utilitarianism cannot both be true, although both could be false.

It may be harder to understand why anyone should be a retributivist than it is to understand the utilitarian position. Who is inclined to say that we should not be concerned to reduce or prevent crime—and that punishment is not an apt means to that end? But are we really entitled to mete out to people what they deserve? Who has a right to do such a thing, even supposing that we can ever know what a person deserves for his acts?

The classic retributivist position is founded on a moral principle: no person should ever be treated as a mere means, but each person should always be treated as an end in herself. To treat a person as a mere means is indefensibly to *use* her: to have no regard for *her* in your undertaking. It is to treat her like a thing, a piece of property, a physical object. But she is entitled to be regarded as a being with her own desires, feelings, and plans. Call this the principle of respect. The principle is clearly articulated in the first of the quotations from Kant.

What, the retributivist asks, can the utilitarian say *to the criminal* in justifying *to her* the treatment that is given her? The retributivist would have to say that she is punishing so that the criminal and other people will be deterred from future crime. But then the criminal can respond, "By punishing me you are using me as a means to your ends. What interests me is my own welfare. I have my own ends and ideals, my own plans, my own direction. You can use me if you will, but don't think that telling me how I am used will justify *to me* the way that you treat me. I don't have to accept your ends, and hence I don't have to accept your reasons for punishing me."[2]

What can the retributivist say, consistently with the principle of respect? The retributivist can argue that to treat the criminal with respect is to assume that he is rational. As rational, he cannot expect that he is entitled to be treated differently from anyone else and that he will be guided by rules that he would be willing for anyone else to follow. But he has killed or injured a person. He therefore has no ground for objection if, like for like, he is in turn killed or injured.

For the retributivist, the principle of respect seems closely associated with another principle, the principle of fairness. That principle requires (minimally) that relevantly like cases be treated alike and relevantly different cases differently. To treat a person as an end in herself, to respect her, is to assume that she is rational. But rational persons accept the principle of fairness. It is irrational to suppose that one can justify a course of action by saying that it is excusable just because the agent is who she is, and that she is therefore entitled to get away with doing what other people may not do. To avoid a punishment that is "equal" to the crime, that consists in treating like cases alike (execution for murder), she would have to repudiate the principle of fairness. If she does that, she is not being rational. If, to respect her, we must assume her rationality, then we must assume that she accepts the principle of fairness.

The principle of respect also demands that we treat the *victim* of the crime with respect. The victim must be assured that what he has suffered matters. Utilitarians would use him, just as they do the criminal, in a consequence-enhancing strategy. But he has been attacked, robbed, beaten, wounded, cheated, hurt. He has been diminished, reduced by being treated as a mere impediment to gain, an insensible object of rage, or a warm body for gratification. Under the principle of respect for persons, we cannot just stand by and do nothing about the particular degradation that the particular victim has suffered. But utilitarian-inspired attempts to seize the occasion of the crime as one on which future crime might be diminished or deterred fail to meet this demand. They are doing something, indeed, but failing to recognize the victim as a human being entitled to respect.

CONCLUSIONS, SO FAR

The main conclusion at which we have arrived is that, while there are reasons for doubting legal punishment can be morally justified, the classic theories that are offered in justification are themselves inconsistent. They cannot both be accepted. (They cannot, that is, unless we agree with Emerson's remark that the fear of inconsistency is the "hobgoblin of little minds"!)

We began by identifying three of the reasons why legal punishment may be considered morally wrong: Criminals are not responsible for their deeds (Owen), punishment cannot be made to square with religious teachings (Tolstoy), and punishment is superfluous, cruel, an indignity, given the torture the criminal inflicts on himself (Dostoyevsky).

We then found that, underlying these objections to legal punishment (which we defined as a particular practice), there is a large moral question. How can we engage morally in a practice of harming people unless we have a very good argument (a justification) for doing so?

Then we discovered that the classic justifications of punishment that have been offered, utilitarian (Bentham and Paley) and retributivist (Kant), are jointly inconsistent. Utilitarians hold that the *only* morally acceptable justification for the practice of punishment (hoped-for good consequences) rests on the principle of utility. Retributivists contend that the *only* acceptable reason for punishment (desert of the criminal) rests on the principles of respect and fairness. Utilitarians and retributivists agree then that punishment can be justified, but both positions cannot be true and both may be false.

Which of these alternative positions, if either, can we accept? If neither is acceptable, where do we go from there in our moral assessment of the practice of punishment?

NOTES

1. The reference here is to those classic utilitarians whose views have been influential in the debate over punishment. There are utilitarians for whom happiness is not the or the only desirable consequence to be maximized.

2. Of course, if the criminal were himself a utilitarian, he would not reason in this way and would accept the proferred justification.

The Dilemma of Punishment

What has gone wrong? Why can't deterrence *and* desert count in justifying punishment? Isn't it because of the *exclusive* claims made for these considerations that there is a conflict? If the retributivist interest in desert rests on the principles of respect and fairness and if the classic utilitarian fixation on deterrence follows from the utilitarian principle that happiness should be maximized, then aren't both theories wrong—wrong in claiming that the opposing principles don't apply in the justification of punishment? The traditional arguments against the two theories suggest that this is so.

THE IMPASSE

First, consider what has often been offered by retributivists as the knock-down argument against utilitarians. It is some version of the charge that to be a utilitarian, a *consistent* one, is to have no concern for fairness or respect. It is argued, for example, that a utilitarian judge would sometimes have to convict and sentence an innocent person. Why? Because if a type of crime is on the rise and it is difficult to find and convict the culprits, and if the judge has before the bar a person whom the judge alone knows is innocent (and whose innocence no one else is ever likely to find out), she will be forced to make an example of this person by severely punishing him. As a consistent utilitarian, the judge must be an opportunist. She must take advantage of every opportunity to increase happiness and decrease misery. Here is an opportunity. Only one person will suffer; the unhappiness of the many who are harmed by crime will be reduced because punishment of the "culprit" will deter other potential culprits.[1]

Suppose that the crime is arson and it is hard to convict clever arsonists. Then, by inflicting the maximum allowable sentence on the "arsonist," the judge saves untold numbers of lives, prevents multiple injuries, and helps protect public and private property. The strength of this antiutilitarian argument is precisely that a consistent utilitarian, like William Paley, must ignore what in fact he says he will ignore: the desert of the accused. In this case, the accused deserves no punishment at all but is being sentenced to be imprisoned. Even if the judge can think of some alternative way of reducing arson, she will seriously have to consider sentencing this innocent man. But surely, says the retributivist, even if the judge should finally not sentence an innocent, this is just an immoral way to *think* about what should be done. Morally speaking, the question should not even arise whether it might be useful to sentence an innocent person.

Can the utilitarian avoid the moral force of this sort of argument? There *is* a move he can make. He can say that what best promotes the public happiness is a system in which judges sentence only those found guilty, a *practice* in which it can be taken for granted that judges will not sentence a person they know to be innocent. According to the practice, only those found guilty *can* be sentenced. If there were no assurance that the finding of guilt would precede sentencing, then what deterrent effect could there be in the threat to make a person miserable if she violates the law? Given the opportunity for crime, a person would not be deterred by the prospect of punishment because she might also be punished if she did not commit the crime.[2] A person peering into a jewelry store window at 3:00 AM might as well break the glass and grab the diamond necklace. So how could a utilitarian favor a *practice* in which judges can punish innocents? (Utilitarians who take this line are called "rule utilitarians." It is for them the set of rules, the practice, that is of primary concern in determining what course of action the consistent utilitarian should follow. He should abide by the rules of a practice that maximizes happiness or, at least, minimizes misery. The rule utilitarian is contrasted with the "act utilitarian" who believes that each of her acts should be happiness-maximizing.)

It is hard to see, though, how this distinction weakens the force of the punishment-of-the-innocent argument, even if it makes for a more defensible overall utilitarian theory. Even supposing it in general true that practices that are in the interest of public happiness should not be undermined or eroded away, how does that relieve the utilitarian judge from thinking only of what best promotes happiness in his resolution of this case? By hypothesis, he alone knows that the accused is innocent and no one else is ever likely to find it out. So undermining or erosion are unlikely or impossible. More generally, it is difficult to understand why a consistent utilitarian should not always have to ask herself what is in the interest of the general happiness—to follow the rules of the practice or to do what in the circumstances leads to most happiness. From her point of view, if following the practice gives results that are fair, that is accidental. Paley's blunt rejection of desert as having any bearing on punishment is a straightforward presentation of the utilitarian position. But if desert is not taken into account, how can punishment be fair? And if it is not fair, how can it evince respect for the criminal?

Classic retributivists, too, are vulnerable. As we have seen, Immanuel Kant is as forthright as Paley in rejecting any and all considerations in justifying punishment but those concerning desert. But if only desert is relevant, what, as retributivists, can we say in justifying a particular sentence? Are we not confined to talking about the heinousness of the criminal's deed? And, for all the talk about respect and fairness, are we not then using the language of revenge? How, if we are retributivists, can we distinguish what we say in justification of a sentence from what Hatfield says in justification of killing a McCoy: "He killed a Hatfield, so we have a right to kill him." Is the language of retribution not just a smooth and sophisticated cover for a morally questionable motive, the motive to take vengeance on the criminal? Are we not entitled to read Kant as saying that people are to be executed or imprisoned even if it will do no good—even if it will do positive harm, as it certainly will to the criminal?

Is there a way out of the impasse? There could be if classic retributivists and utilitarians were not talking about the same thing—were passing each other in the night. If retributivists, say, had in mind judicial discussions of punishment and utilitarians were thinking about legislative ones, then there might be a way out. There is some plausibility in this account of how the dilemma arises. Kant does insist that punishment must be imposed "only because the individual on whom it is inflicted has committed a crime." Paley may be concerned, as Jeremy Bentham certainly was, primarily with the reform of criminal law. So aren't retributivists saying that *judges* should be concerned solely with desert, and aren't utilitarians contending that *legislators* should focus only on the prevention of crime?

Unfortunately, neither classic retributivists nor classic utilitarians are so careful as to restrict their claims to a particular kind of discussion about punishment: judicial or legislative. Even if they were, the restriction would be at best questionable. If judges must consider only desert in sentencing, then they cannot take into account the effect of the sentence they hand down. Yet it is just the hoped-for consequences of a sentence that often seem to justify it. "Shock incarceration," for example, is intended to deter the first-time offender from repetition of crime; or a severe sentence for driving while intoxicated may serve as a message to would-be offenders. Similarly, it is unclear how legislators can rationally be persuaded to ignore the question what persons deserve for a given type of offense when they are discussing the penalties to be attached to crimes. (Whether there is any rational way to calculate what a person deserves is a topic we will take up shortly.)

What seems curious about the argument between classic retributivists and utilitarians is the insistence, on each side, that only one sort of consideration is relevant in the justification of punishment. Why not both sorts? Why can't a person rationally take into account both desert and deterrence? Why isn't the insistence on the exclusive relevance of one sort of consideration just wrong—an indefensible kind of reductivism?

What may be at work is a questionable assumption about the nature of justification. It is that if more than one sort of consideration is allowed as relevant, then we may not be able to weigh considerations against each other in calculating legislative penalties or sentences. Situations may arise in which considerations of desert point in one direction and considerations of deterrence in another. The punishment-of-the-innocent example is a case in point.

Yet to insist that desert cannot be weighed against deterrence is to play the ostrich. Desert and deterrence are in fact weighed every day in court and in legislature, even though there seems to be no formula by means of which they can be reduced to a common scale — a scale that decides in advance for all future cases how they are to be measured one against the other. Retributivists and utilitarians choose too easy a way out. They would have us avoid the problem of weighing by assigning, in advance, absolute weight to one sort of consideration and no weight at all to the other sort.

AN UNDERLYING WEAKNESS IN RETRIBUTIVISM

Yet how can retributivist and utilitarian considerations be meaningfully related to one another? Is there any way of combining them, perhaps with other sorts of consideration, to yield a moral justification of punishment? One way to approach the problem is to ask more exactly how the classic positions fail morally to justify punishment. Perhaps in understanding the sources of their weakness, we can begin to understand how they need amendment (just as in appreciating their strength, we can see where they do not need amendment).

Let us begin with the first retributivist proposition, that the only acceptable reason for punishing a person is that she has committed a crime. As we know, the retributivist wants to insist here on a very tight relation between desert and punishment. It is because the criminal deserves punishment that she is to be punished; she deserves punishment in virtue of what she has done. As we move on to the second and third propositions, we see that punishment must, if morally justified, be warranted by the degree of the criminal's ill desert — the greater the desert, the more onerous the punishment. And we see that it is the desert of the criminal that not only warrants punishment but also makes punishment morally mandatory. There is something morally amiss if the criminal is not punished. The underlying assumption of all of this is that *criminals deserve to be punished*. It will be worth our while to consider that proposition for a few moments.

Because some people are entirely opposed to legal punishment, it may fairly be asked of retributivists what reasons they have for saying that criminals deserve punishment. Paley does not think that desert should be taken into account at all in determining what should be done about crime. What is the argument that criminals deserve punishment? Here we must speculate because our question seems not to be an explicit subject of philosophical discussion. That criminals deserve to be punished is in fact not directly challenged by classic utilitarians. They do not so much raise that question as the question whether, in light of the overwhelming importance of the consequences of punishment in calculating how and how much to punish, we should allow desert any weight on the judicial scales.

Suppose then that the retributivist is challenged to defend his belief that criminals deserve to be punished. How is he to defend it? The first move that he would have to make is to distinguish between what is deserved for legal and for moral guilt. The distinction between legal and moral guilt, which will loom larger later on in our discussion, is not an easy one to make, but it can be illustrated by examples. In *Les Misérables*, Victor Hugo invents a character who is, through no fault of his own, in desperate straits and who steals a loaf of bread to feed his family. If he is caught, it is natural to say that, even though he is legally guilty of theft, he is not morally guilty. Or consider the newspaper editor under a Latin American dictatorship who defies the law to publish a story about government corruption. Because the retributivist's position would be but trivially true if he were insisting merely that the existence of a system of criminal law implies a meaningful threat to punish, we must assume that he wants to make a more substantive claim. He must want to assert that the morally guilty should be punished — punished in accordance with their moral deserts. He must be thinking of the criminal law as a social device to ensure that moral guilt meets its due. That this is what Kant, at least, believes is evident from our quotations in Chapter 1.[3]

Let us leave aside the question of how it would be possible to have a system of law in which all and only the morally guilty were punished. Let us focus on the underlying retributive moral position: The morally guilty deserve punishment. Here we must distinguish two possible interpretations. The retributivist could be saying that, in a system in which criminals are either to undergo behavior modification (or some other mode of compelling them to be law-abiding) or to be punished, criminals deserve punishment rather than behavior modification. Or, second, she could be saying, as Kant seems to, that systems of law should be designed in such a way that all and only the morally guilty are punished. On the first interpretation, the insistence that criminals be punished is equally an insistence that they not be merely manipulated, made pliable to the demands of law, as if they had no wills or minds of their own. This insistence could quite intelligibly be related to the demand that the criminal be treated with respect, as an end in himself, and not as a mere means to the achievement of some state of affairs that he may or may not approve. (This is qualified by Kant's notion that once punishment is justified by desert the overall good may be taken into account in determining what nonpunishment measures should be taken with respect to the criminal.)

The second interpretation is for us the centrally important one: that those and only those should be punished who morally deserve punishment. The insistence on matching punishment to desert could be on fairness in the application of law to particular cases. But the retributivist cannot merely be insisting on equal treatment under the law, that lawbreakers be treated impartially. Utilitarians can easily agree that a fairly administered system of law is a more effective one. But this uncontroversial proposition cannot be what the retributivist means to assert. What is in this sense fair, that is, equitable under the given rules of law and judicial procedure, is not necessarily what is morally deserved. The rules of a legal system can be radically at odds with common intuitions about what people morally deserve.

The retributivist must be presupposing something about moral desert then: that it exists quite independently of fairness under a given legal system. There is intuitive evidence for such a claim. We seem to be able to say with assurance that, whatever a legal system may hold, the person who tortures and kills another person deserves worse than a person who merely steals another's property. But worse what, and at whose hands? What is the argument that she *deserves to be punished*? We may say of the boy who slips on the banana peel he has maliciously thrown on the sidewalk, or of the crooked promoter who loses money in his own scheme, that they deserve "what they got." We have terms for that sort of thing: "cosmic" or "poetic" justice;[4] and we know how to distinguish these sorts of "comeuppances" from legal punishment. The retributivist may want to say then that legal punishment for wrongdoing is deserved to whatever extent the punishment is in accord with cosmic justice. This response leaves open the question, "What entitles us to attempt to enforce cosmic justice through our legal system?"

Until the retributivist provides us with a satisfactory answer, her position is seriously flawed. If there is no good answer, then our doubts about retributivism must extend beyond worries about the retributivist claim that only considerations of desert are relevant in the justification of punishment. We must now wonder how the retributivist can use claims about what a person cosmically deserves for doing what is morally wrong to justify inflicting legal punishment on him — even supposing that we could determine the kind and degree of punishment that is appropriate to cosmic desert.

The problem is one of moral standing to punish. A comeuppance, the slip on the banana peel, can be viewed in two ways: as a mere contingent event, an accident, or as a result from the intervention of some Higher Power. If it is a contingent event, there is no inflicter of punishment, and the issue of standing does not arise. The problem of God's standing to inflict punishment is a distinct one from that of the moral standing of human agents of a legal system. It is better left to theology. If the retributivist claims standing to punish as an agent of God-administered cosmic justice, that assumption should be made explicit.

UTILITARIAN WEAKNESSES

Let us now turn to a closer examination of the classic utilitarian position on punishment, the position that we may summarize as claiming that it is only the deterrent value of punishment that can justify a given mode and degree of punishment. Here we must bear in mind that the utilitarian does not insist on punishment as *the* (or even as *a*) remedy for crime. Since her overall objective is increased public happiness and decreased public misery and because punishment by its nature will create some misery, the misery of the criminal, the utilitarian must favor remedies, if any, that have a lower "cost" in misery. To assess thoroughly the classic utilitarian position on legal punishment then, we would have to take up the general theory that the "greatest happiness of the greatest number" should govern all our actions and policies before we could consider the application of that theory to the question of what to do about crime.

If we were to attempt a general appraisal of classic utilitarianism — too large an undertaking here — we would have to focus on the concept of happiness and of how, on what grounds, we could argue that this or that policy or practice is "for the happiness of the greatest number." Would we be talking about the median or the average happiness of the population? What population would we be talking about? Does it include people outside our own particular national boundaries? If not, on what utilitarian grounds could noncitizens be excluded? How would the intensity of happiness be taken into account? Would short-term intense happiness for an individual cancel long-term, low-level misery? Would very intense happiness on the part of a few persons make up for misery on the part of many? In general, what could we say, as utilitarians, about how happiness should ideally be distributed across a population? Would not justice have to be taken into account in distributing the means to happiness? But how can there be room for justice in a system in which the only relevant considerations concern the happiness of the greatest number? Would "satisfaction" do as a substitute for happiness? Can satisfaction be measured?

Some modern utilitarians adopt a more abstract position than the insistence on the sole relevance of a certain kind of consideration — the maximization of happiness and minimization of misery. They speak not of these particular kinds of consequences of policies and actions but of consequences in general. These "consequentialists" hold that it is solely good or bad consequences that should be taken into account in determining, for example, what should be done about crime. This leaves open the question of how good consequences are to be distinguished from bad ones — how, that is, to produce an alternative consequence to public happiness that will avoid the difficulties apparent in the questions, asked in the preceding paragraph, about the concept of happiness.

The weakness of the retributivist position then appears to center in the undefended presupposition that desert justifies punishment. Utilitarianism's weakness is of another sort. Although we may question whether consequences (especially the particular consequences having to do with public happiness and misery) are the sole considerations relevant to the justification of punishment, as utilitarians claim, still it seems intuitively right to say that consequences *are* morally relevant. They are relevant to the question whether the practice of punishment should be adopted and to questions about the punishment of particular criminals under the practice. The central problem for utilitarians seems be how to reduce a plausible abstract principle — that good or bad consequences should govern our decisions — to morally acceptable specifications of that principle. As soon as utilitarians say what kind or kinds of consequences are to have sole relevance, how they are to be measured, by what methods they are to be encouraged, and to whom they are to apply, great difficulties arise. In particular, the difficulty arises that considerations dear to retributivists must now somehow be shown to be derivable from calculations of consequence. It can be doubted whether that has ever satisfactorily been done.

CAN RETRIBUTIVISM BE SALVAGED?

If there is to be reconciliation between retributivists and utilitarians, it must rest on a reconstruction of those positions that shores up the underlying weaknesses we have discovered. Otherwise, if punishment is to be morally justifiable at all, the justification cannot rest, even partially, on either of the standard theories. Is there a statement of the retributivist position that avoids the questionable underlying assumption about cosmic desert of punishment? Can utilitarians lay down some satisfactory criterion of what is to count as the relevant sort of consequence?

As we noticed in passing, there is an understanding of desert, closely allied to fairness, that the classic retributivist bypasses in favor of a conception of desert as existing "out there" independently of a system of law. On the conception of desert as fairness under a system of law, the idea is that laws should be fair, laws should be fairly administered, and what a person deserves is determined by the fairness of laws and of their administration. On this understanding of desert, it cannot meaningfully be asked, granted a fair system of law and fair application of the law to a particular case, whether the resulting award or sentence is what the person "really" deserves.

Can the fairness or unfairness of a law be understood in some way that does not presuppose the existence of cosmic desert? To understand the fairness of a law in this way, it is necessary to think about the purpose of the law. If we do not know what purpose the law is to serve, we have no way of determining whether the burdens and privileges it creates are fair. Absent a defensible purpose, how are we to answer the complaint of a person who says that he should not have to suffer imprisonment for violating one of the rules of the system? He is asking for a rationale that does not exist. But if he is told that he "just deserves" the imprisonment, he may understandably question whether there is a purpose in the laws. There must be a morally defensible answer we can give the criminal then that does not appeal to cosmic desert (and, hence, to cosmic justice).

A proposal of this kind would have to offer at least some suggestion of how we are to determine that a law is fair.[5] One answer might be that a law is fair when (1) the burdens and privileges it creates can be shown to be necessary or desirable means to the common good and (2) when they are distributed in a way that is likely to serve the common good. However, it is easy to see that the retributivist will, so far, be unwilling to accept this definition of a fair law, even if she has set aside her previous assumption about cosmic justice. She won't willingly accept it because there is so far no protection for the individual person against his being made a "mere means" to however desirable an end. For example, it could be (and has been) claimed that a system of law under which human beings can be the property of other human beings is in the interest of the common good. Under such a system, to help a piece of property, a slave, to escape from his owner is a criminal offense. Such a law can be fairly administered, in the sense that all slave-aiders are equally punished. It will therefore be necessary to add a proviso: (3) The laws must, in promoting the common good, give full weight to the interests of the individuals falling under them.

What a criminal deserves then would be fair treatment under a fair system of laws. An advantage of the conception of desert as fair treatment under fair law is that it reserves a clear place, as cosmic desert does not, for comparative arguments about desert. What a person cosmically deserves seems to be a matter of unsupported intuition, whereas the fairness of laws and their administration are more amenable to comparative analysis. The boundaries of relevance in such debates seem to be more clearly defined than disputes over what people "really" deserve in some abstract context in which laws and their administration have no place.[6] Whether retributivism understood in this way can be reconciled with the utilitarian view of punishment remains to be seen.

CAN PUNISHMENT BE MATCHED TO DESERT?

Even supposing some such analysis of desert were satisfactory, there would still remain the question of whether there is a way to measure the criminal's desert so that we could say with some assurance that one sentence is consistent with his desert while another is not. One of the sources of suspicion of retributivism is precisely that there seems to be no such way—that retributive "reasoning" about such matters is really the rationalization of the desire to take revenge on the criminal. Can conclusions concerning the punishment a criminal deserves be shown to be true? In approaching that question it will be well to look more carefully at the problem of apportioning punishment to crime.

We begin by distinguishing between the legislative and judicial problems of matching punishment to crime. The legislative problem is to establish a scale of crimes and a coordinated scale of punishments. The judicial task is to apply legislatively ordained punishments to particular criminals. The judge may have more or less discretion in matching punishment to crime, as the legislation is less or more specific.

Suppose that the legislature of a new country, drawing up a criminal code for the first time, now has established a scale of crimes from the least to the most serious. Let us say that the scale runs from 1 for the least to 10 for the most serious sorts of crime. We may imagine that littering falls in the first category and premeditated homicide in the last. Let us now add that the legislature has agreed on a scale of punishments that also runs from 1 to 10, 1 being the least severe and 10 the most. For simplicity suppose that the punishment scale ranges from one to ten years' imprisonment. We have now, if we are legislators, the task of relating these two scales one to the other. While it may seem straightforward enough — one year for littering and ten years for premeditated murder — there are reasons to pause over the intermediate positions.

We should first notice that, while the scale of crimes is an ordinal one, the scale of punishments is cardinal. An ordinal scale merely establishes an order between the items to be ranked. For example, an ordinal scale of hardness is established by the scratch test. If material A scratches material B, then it is higher on the scale of hardness than B. By the test, anthracite coal is harder than limestone, and diamonds are harder than anthracite coal. If we assign numbers 1, 2, and 3 to diamonds, anthracite, and limestone, respectively, the numbers could as well be letters. They indicate mere relative position on the scale: which item is "higher" according to some criterion and which is "lower." The scale of crimes, being an ordinal one, exhibits an order of seriousness. But the order is not a calculative one in the sense that, if one crime is in Group 2 and another in Group 6, the first crime is one-third as serious as the second. Cardinal scales are in that sense calculative. A sentence of two years is one-third of a sentence of six years. So we must, if we are to use punishments like imprisonment or fines, relate an ordinal to a cardinal scale.

The interscalar problem is twofold. First (the anchoring problem), we must find a place on each scale where, in some meaningful way, the punishment matches the crime. Without that we have no way of beginning. While we can know that first-degree murder should be higher on the scale of crimes than manslaughter and that x plus one years of imprisonment is a more severe punishment than x years, none of this tells us what we should substitute for x if punishment is to match desert. In addition, a second problem (the interval problem) arises: Because an ordinal scale establishes only an order and if we rank crimes in order of seriousness, we still do not know anything about the size of the intervals between the crimes on the scale.

There are two aspects of the interval problem. First, we will not know how to group crimes into ten groups of ascending seriousness because we won't have any measure of the relative seriousness of the crimes within a group. How are we to know that the most serious crime in Group 6 is not *far* more serious than any other crime in the same group? Second, we won't know how to judge whether the gap between groups of crimes is greater or smaller than an equal gap, so that the ascent in seriousness between Group 4 crimes and Group 5 crimes might be much greater than the gap, say, between Groups 5 and 6. Given this possible disparity of intervals, it seems simply arbitrary to move up the (supposedly) corresponding scale of punishments by a regular interval of one year in determining what the difference should be between punishment for Group 4 and Group 5 crimes.

Should we conclude then that there is no possibility of determining what a given crime deserves on any other ground than impulse, hunch, or intuition? Despite the difficulties noted, a case can be made for the possibility of rational determination of what a criminal deserves. Remember that, as we are now understanding it, desert of a criminal is fair treatment under fair laws. To say that we can't determine desert rationally is to say that we don't know how to decide when a sentence, under fair laws, is fair. But surely we do sometimes know the difference between a fair and an unfair sentence. We know that, if relevantly similar cellmates in the state penitentiary have committed robbery under relevantly similar circumstances and if one is serving a sentence of one year and the other a sentence of ten years, somebody has been unfairly sentenced.

The interscalar problems are, by and large, problems that would arise were the aim the exact determination of desert. But if the aim is the more modest one that there should be a reasonable proportion between what a person has done and what she suffers for it, the difficulties might prove more tractable. It may be that while there are (nonretributive) advantages in fine judgments concerning *punishments*, judgments of *desert* cannot be so finely determined. We cannot calculate desert. But rational determination need not be modeled on calculative models. Appraisals can also be rational.

In saying that B deserves a given sentence in virtue of what he has done, we may be *appraising* B's action in a certain way. We make a claim concerning what is due B, in consequence of the action. (I speak here, for simplicity, of desert for action, although there can be criminal desert for what a person did not do as well— negligence cases often turn on irresponsible *in*action, for example.) In appraising a person's desert, we need to know the factual details of what he has done, and we need facts that help us determine the degree to which what he has done is *his*, reveals him, and is not merely something that has happened to or through him. But the facts do not entail an appraisal any more than the square footage of a house and its location entail its value. Judgment is required; the facts are there to be used but do not, when taken together, yield a judgment.

If we think of judgments of what a person deserves as appraisals, something is revealed about the nature of the considerations that back such judgments. They provide information not only about the criminal herself (for example, she robbed a bank) but also about the circumstances of the act (she was forced to participate). That is, appraisals provide information about the deed and the degree to which the deed is fully the criminal's—for what she is thus fully responsible. If there is to be an appraisal of desert, more is needed than these action-describing and responsibility-revealing considerations because appraisals are inherently comparative. Desert not only admits of rewards and punishments but also of kind and degree. We can ask *what* a person deserves, and, if she deserves what admits of degrees, how much she deserves. We can ask these latter questions, that is, *given that appraisals are to be made*. Given the need to appraise, they can be forced on us, *even when there seems to be no easy way of answering them* or even when any answer given will be to some degree arbitrary. Arbitrariness is not inconsistent here with rational defensibility.

Comparison with another type of appraisal may be useful. In appraising a house, an appraiser must first establish a relevant description, both accurate and properly qualified. Not only must he determine the square footage, damage, deterioration, and so on but he also must qualify his description in such a way that none of these facts will, taken alone, be misleading about the true state of the house. The qualifications are intended to make the description germane to the appraisal. Thus, a part of the square footage is in an unfinished wing, the tornado damage is superficial, or the deterioration of the foundation is serious. This qualified description establishes the groundwork for an appraisal, as does the qualified description of an act. The qualifications that are relevant to the appraisal of an act help us determine to what extent the act, as a physical event, reveals the true nature of the agent's action. We are thus interested in questions—such as those concerning accident, provocation, or insanity—that hedge or cancel more directly descriptive matters, such as the presence or absence of a weapon.

But given this hedged or qualified description of what happened and that what did happen constitutes under the law a crime, the appraisal of desert remains to be made. An appraisal is a comparative judgment, and a comparative basis must be established. The appraiser of houses must determine values of comparable houses by recent sales prices. But if there are no recent sales, she must use whatever evidence, however tangential, is available. We may think of judgments of desert in an analagous way.

If, as we have suggested, they are equivalent to judgments of what is fair under a fair system of laws, it may still be difficult to establish a basis of comparison. To say that the determination of desert for crime, whether legislative or judicial, can be rationally grounded is not to say that it is simple or easy to decide what a criminal deserves for his crime. Still, supposing that there is some nonretributive reason for punishing, there is moral force to the demand that people should be punished fairly. If desert can be tied to fairness, there may be hope for resolving the classic impasse over the grounds for legal punishment.

| CONCLUSION

The impasse between classic retributivists and utilitarians rests on the exclusive claim that each theory makes for the relevance of considerations peculiar to the theory. Classic retributivists refuse to accept considerations of utility, whereas classic utilitarians do not accept references to desert as relevant to the justification of punishment. The problem then is to determine the way in which each of these admittedly relevant kinds of consideration can be combined into a consistent argument for the practice of punishment. The approach is to examine the weaknesses in retributive and utilitarian theories. This survey leads to the conclusion that reconciliation can start with reconstruction of the retributive theory by redefining desert as what is owed under fair administration of fair laws. The utilitarian theory is more persuasive at the abstract level than it is in specifying the kinds of consequence that are to be solely relevant. We begin with the utilitarian's problem in Chapter 3, in which we ask how the practice of punishment might be morally justified.

NOTES

1. In most criminal trials today, the jury determines guilt. This traditional argument would be greatly complicated were we required to imagine a utilitarian jury composed of the only persons who knew, or were ever likely to know, that the accused was innocent! Nevertheless, the argument does underline the point that a consistent utilitarian can grant no independent weight to considerations of justice. To have weight in utilitarian calculations, an appeal to justice must be an indirect appeal to good consequences, as would be the case were the jury foreman to argue that potential criminals might be better deterred if the sentence were, or anyway seemed, just.

2. John Rawls (1955) suggests that, to avoid confusion, we should not speak of a practice in which a judge may arbitrarily inflict misery on an accused as punishment. We might, he suggests, call it "telishment," and speak of "telishing" rather than punishing.

3. If this is the position, then the question arises how to draw the line between the moral guilt that should and should not be punishable under the law. Should the ungrateful, for example, be tried and sentenced? We will discuss that question in Chapter 12.

4. John Kleinig (p. 51) introduces the term "raw desert" to indicate the desert that "cosmic" or "poetic" justice would punish. I use the term "cosmic desert."

5. The criterion or criteria of fairness are subjects of dispute in political and legal philosophy. What follows relies on a widely held conception of that difficult notion.

6. Note that the conception of desert as fair treatment under fair laws is still a rather narrow one because what is at issue is only criminal desert. By substituting "rules" for "laws" and understanding rules broadly enough to incorporate common understandings and moral injunctions about what is or is not permissible in a community, the conception of desert introduced here could be broadened. An appropriately broad conception could encompass many of the judgments about desert that at first sight might seem to be merely intuitive assessments of cosmic desert. On either the narrow or the broad conception, however, fairness will be seen to imply consequential reasoning, as we suggest in the next section.

Can Punishment Be Justified?

The difficulty with the utilitarian position remains: It must specify which sort of consequence is to have sole relevance in justifying punishment. However, we have not found cause to reject the position that consequences *should* be taken into account when there is a question whether and how a criminal should be punished. In fact, we have seen the emergence, if desert is understood as fair treatment under fair rules, of a role for utilitarian considerations in the justification of punishment. This role possibly may be acceptable to retributivists, for it is unclear how a set of laws that penalizes persons uselessly, to no purpose, can be fair. An obvious way to introduce purpose is to point to hoped-for good effects of penal legislation.

THE POSSIBILITY OF RECONCILIATION

The suggested reconciliation would require the retributivist to accept the following argument:

1. Criminals should be punished only in accordance with their desert.

2. What criminals deserve is fair treatment under fair laws.

3. A criminal law is unfair if, for no good purpose, it inflicts suffering or loss on criminals while other persons are not so inflicted.

4. The expectation of good consequences or the avoidance of bad ones counts as a good purpose.

5. Thus, consequences are relevant to the justification of punishment.[1]

The retributivist might object that a legal system that attempts to match punishment to desert *is* a nonconsequential purposive one; the purpose is to give people what they deserve. However, this answer presupposes several questionable beliefs: that there is cosmic desert; that there is an intelligible and morally acceptable set of criteria for the determination of what lawbreakers cosmically deserve; and that anyone but God has moral standing to enforce cosmic justice.

The suggestion was made that laws cannot be fair that sacrifice the interests of groups falling under the law. This is a difficult conception to make clear. But it seems to say, at least, that the laws in question do not punish or otherwise burden individuals who fall under them without good reason. That would put burdened people at an unfair disadvantage compared with those who are not burdened.

Colonel Blimp might say that all that a peasant has a right to complain about is that she is not treated equally, under penal law, with other peasants. The peasant has no right, that is, to question whether there are reasons for having the penalties in the first place. But the peasant might understandably feel that she is being treated unfairly if there are no acceptable reasons for the penalty she suffers. What would be acceptable reasons? It is difficult to articulate a general answer to this question. At the same time, it is easy to understand that the peasant will rightly feel that she is unfairly treated if her interests are a naught in the calculation of costs and benefits—that while the interests of the gentry are protected, the peasants' interests are ignored.

Suppose that the colonel, as administrator, issues an edict that swimming in the village pond will henceforth be a capital offense; and suppose that the only swimmers in the pond, from time immemorial, have been peasants (the gentry being well supplied with private ponds). Suppose that Blimp gives no reason at all for this edict, or that he says that it interferes with the afternoon nap of his pet turtle, or that peasants are a worthless lot and don't deserve to enjoy themselves. We may safely assume that the peasants will feel that they have been treated unfairly and, further, that they are justified in feeling as they do. Examples of this kind can be multiplied to make clear that even though there may be difficulty in articulating a theory that defines acceptable reasons, we can recognize unacceptable ones.

More generally, one way to make clear the nature of fairness in the laws might be to start from paradigm cases of unfair laws and ask whether there were relevant analogies with the laws under examination. Then fair laws would be those that were not relevantly analogous to the paradigmatically unfair ones. Theory would then start from the attempt to specify what did and did not count as a relevant analogy and why.

So far the suggestion is that, when the weaknesses in the classic theories of punishment are shored up and the theories made defensible, they begin to find a fit with each other. If retributivism is the contention that punishment is justified only when people are treated fairly under fair laws and if utilitarianism is only the claim that the effects of punishment must necessarily be taken into account in justifying punishment, there is a possible fit. There is a possible fit because there can be no fair laws in the absence of a justifiable purpose in the infliction of burdens on those who fall under them. The price traditional theorists would have to pay for this possibility of reconciliation is abandonment of their use of the word *only*. They can no longer claim that *only* retributive or *only* utilitarian considerations are relevant in the justification of punishment.

But even supposing that the traditional positions can be reconciled, we have still not faced up to the problem of the justification of legal punishment. Why need there be any such practice as legal punishment? Unless the practice is justified, the suffering we inflict on criminals, like suffering inflicted on anyone, is morally wrong. How then, if at all, can punishment be justified?

ONE APPROACH TO THE JUSTIFICATION OF PUNISHMENT

What *is* the purpose or what are the purposes, if any, of the practice of legal punishment? Is it or are they morally acceptable? If we could be clear about the answers to those questions, then we could ask the crucial moral question, "Is there any alternative practice to punishment, an alternative way of serving the same purpose, that is morally preferable to punishment?" Is there some set of circumstances that makes it necessary or desirable to have *some* practice or practices, among which punishment is one option?

Suppose we start, with utilitarians, by saying that the purpose of punishment is to reduce crime.[2] This may be a more plausible beginning than saying, with retributivists, that the purpose is to give criminals their due. The latter answer seems to rest on beliefs about cosmic desert that we have found reason to question. But our answer assumes that we know what is to count as crime, that punishment is an effective means of reducing it, and that of the effective crime-reducing practices available punishment is at least as morally defensible as any of the others.

What then are we to understand by crime? To answer that question, we are forced to step back and consider what might be called the rationale of rules. If we think of crime as, whatever else it may be, the violation of rules[3] and if we think that we are morally permitted to punish those violations, then we must say what it is about rules that makes their defense (by means of the threat of punishment) morally desirable.

To argue that rules are in themselves desirable would be absurd. No one, we assume, wants rules for the sake of the rules themselves, especially rules that carry with them a penalty for their violation. On the other hand, few people would deny some value to rules. Their value lies in the social role they can play. To understand that role fully, we would have to examine some assumptions on which the case for rules must rest. Among the assumptions in question would be those concerning human society, human nature, and nature.

Suppose we assume, in thinking about the value of rules (in particular, penalty-backed rules) that were social life not rule-governed it would be intolerable. (This may be a conceptual truth. Would we count anything as a society in which there were no rules?) We assume that in the absence of rules there could be no property, no contracts, no security, no possibility of planning for the future, no assurance on which side of the road we should drive, or that red lights mean something different from green ones. We assume that certain features of our common life are valuable: our physical security, the institution of property, the practice of making contracts and less formal agreements, the possibility of making plans with some assurance of how others will act in the future. We assume, in short, that were there no rules there would be no boundaries on permitted behavior, no practices essential for our common well-being, no chance of making plans based on predictions of or trust in the behavior of others. Life without rules would be chaotic and unstructured, intolerably dangerous and miserable.

To support this conclusion, we need not speculate about what life would be like in a "state of nature." We need only imagine life in the absence of rules that lay out the minimal boundaries of acceptable behavior, in other words, of the criminal law. In such a life, there would be the continual fear of attack, injury, or death. That is, we would fear these things given yet another assumption about human nature—that humans are, by and large, motivated by self-interest. This is not only to say that they (or dangerous minorities of them) are not (or are seldom) altruistic. But it is also to say that humans are not neutral between their own interests and those of others. We cannot therefore leave it to the workings of natural instincts to create and maintain a tolerable common life. We must introduce into human society some social device that will take advantage of this tendency of the human animal to pursue its own perceived interest and that will make use of that motive for desirable ends. We must, in short, substitute for the instinct of the ant and the bee—social creatures, too—a threat that unless certain rules are respected consequences will follow that are *not* in the interest of the violator, the criminal.

Let us speculate even further. Besides these assumptions about human society and human nature, it is necessary, if we are to offer a rationale of rules—in particular, a system of criminal laws—that we add an assumption about nature. Worlds are conceivable in which, although rules might be desirable or necessary, it would not be necessary to provide any penalty for their violation. In one such world, natural or supernatural forces might be so arranged that the mere adoption by society of a rule would cause those falling under the rule to obey it. By this happy coincidence between nature and the social order, as soon as a potential thief makes a move toward a tempting pocketbook, an irresistible force (physical or psychological) carries him away in the opposite direction, perhaps in the direction of a consoling tavern. In another such world, no natural or supernatural force prevents crime, but a force visits instant retribution on criminals. No sooner has a miscreant seized a purse than she is struck down by lightning. No sooner does a counterfeiter mail his order for a printing press than he comes down with the plague.

Given these assumptions then, there would follow the necessity of rules and of some social device that encourages general compliance with them. At this point, the argument for legal punishment turns to a comparison of the advantages and disadvantages and the moral defensibility or indefensibility of alternative social devices—and to the question whether, given these alternative means of supporting a system of rules, punishment should be retained or abolished. Although no such survey can yield a conclusive argument that punishment is or is not an eliminable practice, still it does provide an intelligible means of appreciating the relative merits of that practice—relative, that is, to the merits of other possible practices. What might some of those practices be?

Inevitably, the choice we make of practices for dealing with crime reflects our assumptions about the nature and causes of the violation of rules. Consider violations of the rule against killing. If we think of the murderer as diseased, then she will need a course of treatment. If she is merely confused or mistaken in her beliefs about what is permissible, we have to institutionalize means of convincing her that murder is wrong. If murder is the consequence of social pressures, we have to ease or rearrange those pressures. If murder results from hidden psychological tangles, then we have to devise means of detecting and unraveling them. If murderers are genetically determined to kill, then we need a means of identifying and guarding against those whose unfortunate inheritance is that dangerous tendency. These assumptions imply different conclusions about responsibility for crime. This is a subject that we reserve for later. Here it is enough if we succeed in enlarging the frame within which we examine the practice of legal punishment.

To see punishment in this larger perspective is to recognize it as but one practice among others for encouraging compliance with rules. Were we to generate arguments about the merits of this or that practice, taken as the sole means to that end, we would have lost sight of the problem of how viable and morally acceptable practices might be reconciled. In the interest of justifying the practice of punishment, it would be absurd to suppose that we must show that there is no merit in reform of the social conditions that make murder more likely or that there is no need to determine what particular psychological traits are associated with lethal violence.

It would be equally absurd to discount in advance any educational programs that might reduce the incidence of murder and other crimes. The problem of the justification of punishment is not one of exhibiting that practice's exclusive claims to adoption but of showing that it is one among the acceptable practices for dealing with the problem of noncompliance with socially necessary rules. Punishment and these other practices may be complementary rather than mutually exclusive. The question is whether, given our assumptions and granted the social necessity not just of rules but of rules that are followed with some reasonable consistency, the practice of punishment is eliminable.

What would a world be like in which there were no legal punishment, supposing that there were legal rules with nonpunishing practices for encouraging compliance? Before answering that question, we have to make some predictions about matters of fact. We have to assess the chances of educational, psychological, and sociological means of reducing crime. To do that and to be able to assess better the acceptability of those means, we need some detail about the practices in question. It is perfectly conceivable that there could be practices that are nearly perfectly effective in reducing crime, but which we nevertheless reject on other grounds. A refractory population could be tranquilized by drugging the public-water supply or made averse to crime by enforced behavioral conditioning. Yet it is far from clear that we would willingly choose such a world in preference to a more dangerous world in which there were no such practices. But it hardly needs arguing that there are alternatives to punishment that, although not perfectly effective, are at once useful and morally acceptable. To whatever extent education, treatment, or positive reinforcement can discourage crime, they are to be welcomed.

Still, whatever practices we may adopt for the reduction of crime, there seems to be good reason to make fallback provision for punishment. Whereas other practices rest on the hope of reforming or otherwise changing the individual or the social order, punishment accepts that a socially malign self-interest may well continue to be a part of human motivation. Thus, no matter what other practices we may adopt for the purpose of minimizing crime, we could not lightly abandon a practice that makes it in the self-interest of the person contemplating a crime not to commit it. That is one argument for legal punishment. We should be reluctant to abandon punishment so long as we believe that, no matter what other crime-reducing measures are taken, there will continue to be tension between rules and the perceived self-interest of persons falling under them. The argument assumes that the threat of punishment is taken seriously and is capable of influencing the potential criminal's choice whether to commit a crime. These are large assumptions and are subject to question in different circumstances. For example, if there is lax enforcement, the potential criminal may well calculate that he stands to gain more by violating the law than by abiding by it. The threat of punishment must have weight at the hour of temptation.

A second argument, one that involves more the question of moral acceptability than of effectiveness, is that, unlike conditioning or treatment, punishment does not leave aside the question of individual responsibility for crime. It is not merely a device for reduction or control but is also a practice that leaves choice open to the person contemplating crime. If to commit a crime is simply to do what is prohibited by the criminal law, then occasions may well arise on which the individual decides, quite defensibly, to commit a crime. She may decide that she should steal to feed a starving family, that she should lie down across the access gate to a nuclear plant, that she should sit on the front seat of a segregated bus, or that she should disconnect the mechanisms sustaining the life of a terminally ill, comatose patient.

Also, even supposing that the crime she commits is not defensible but is atrociously bad, it is arguable that she has chosen not only the act but the punishment that follows the act. Punishment operates like a reverse-pricing system, the idea being to discourage the "buyer" from "buying" anything at all, especially the more "expensive" items. Given a system of this kind, the justification of the particular measures taken against a criminal do not rest entirely on the advantage to the community—as conditioning and treatment are likely to do—but also on the choice that the criminal has made. This is a point that we have noticed in our discussion of the retributivist position.

So much then for the hoped-for good consequences of the practice of punishment and for the abstract context on which the argument rests. However, even if, in the abstract, the practice of punishment can be shown to have a place in an effective and morally acceptable system of rules, problems remain with its justification. The quarrel with punishment now descends to the question, "Which, if any, variety of that practice can be justified?" If there are morally decisive objections to all viable options for punishing people, then the defense of punishment will have failed. Although the forms of punishment have ranged from transportation to hanging and from the stocks to burning at the stake, they reduce in most Western nations to three: imprisonment, capital punishment, and fines. We therefore confine our discussion to those three.

IMPRISONMENT, CAPITAL PUNISHMENT, AND FINES

As any reader of the daily newspapers knows, there are problems with imprisonment as it is practiced in the United States. The prison population is large and growing. Since 1980 the number of adults behind bars has doubled. In 1989 there were more inmates in state and federal prisons, 627,000, than there were inhabitants of the cities of Denver, New Orleans, or Washington, D. C. The conditions of life in crowded federal and state penitentiaries, to say nothing of county jails and city lock-ups, have been the subject of many studies. It is fair to summarize that imprisonment in this country too often means subjection to indignities, the possibility of severe injury or loss of life, and increased motivation toward criminal behavior.

In the state of Texas alone in 1985, twenty-seven prisoners in the state prison system were killed in prison violence. This does not count the persons killed in county jails or the persons injured, raped, or tortured. The mistreatment of prisoners at the hands of other prisoners is certainly not included in the sentence passed down by the judge. No judge includes in his sentence convict-administered injury, rape, or violent death. But this is what sentence to imprisonment too often means.

Prisons are expensive. Currently, the average cost per year per offender is $25,000. Because voter pressure for expenditures on prisons seldom matches voter interest in sending criminals to prison, legislators are reluctant to appropriate the funds necessary for keeping up with the flow of convicted felons. Sheer economics has led, in consequence of the shortage of prison funds, to some reforms: suspended sentences, enforced service to the community, the shortening of sentences, the increased use of probation and parole, and the building of community-based centers in which prisoners live at night but are released for gainful employment during the day. It ought to be obvious, in any case, that reforms justified on economic grounds are often morally mandatory. Even if, ideally, imprisonment can be fair, respectful of the person imprisoned, and sympathetic to the interests of everyone concerned, it is too often, under present conditions, none of these things.

If the object is to reduce crime, we can take it for granted that the best course is to restore to health the sickly conditions that generate crime as surely as polluted water generates disease. We must bring into clear focus the situation of people who enter adolescence and maturity in hopelessness and frustration. We must probe the social and psychological mechanisms that cause "inexplicable" violence. We must carefully analyze the distortions of reason and motivation that make crime, even the most violent, seem not only acceptable but even admirable. But none of this comes to grips with the immediate problem at hand. That problem starts with the commission of crime, the presence before the bar of the convicted criminal, and asks "What now?" What practice will we follow in dealing with convicted criminals? Given the alternatives—alternatives that do not, because this is a case of crime already committed, include methods that rely on forehanded means of reducing the incidence of crime—it seems difficult to dismiss imprisonment as an option. The criminal may be dangerous. She may need to be deterred from future crime. She should perhaps be shown that breaking the law has costs. It seems unjust that she should go unscathed, given what her victim has suffered. Imprisonment is a punishment that can in principle satisfy all these implicit or explicit demands.

Need imprisonment suffer from the defects that too often today characterize it? Perhaps not. *Shock incarceration* is a punitive device that supposedly shortens and improves the effectiveness of imprisonment, at least for young offenders.

> Five young men—three burglars, an arsonist and a car thief—arrived at the Dodge Correctional Institute . . . with long hair, designer jeans, tattoos and an attitude of independent swagger. In short order the swagger was gone. Their hair was shorn to a nub. Their clothes, jewelry and cigarette lighters disappeared into gray plastic bags. Stripped, showered, and deloused, they were ordered into the baggy, impersonal uniforms of prison and formed a line in front of Lieut. James Combs, a former Army drill instructor. . . . "Hold your head up" he barked. "Make believe you are somebody." That was their welcome to a Georgia program meant to give young criminals a tough 90-day experience of prison life that they will never wish to repeat.[4]

In Japan where prison terms are comparatively short, well-trained guards are very tough but strictly fair. Prisoner harrassment of prisoner is extremely rare. Fewer than 4 percent of the prisoners are sentenced for longer than three years. In the United States, 80 percent of those in state institutions have been sentenced for longer than five years.

Experience suggests that shorter and better supervised terms are possible and desirable, that the conditions and deterrent effectiveness of prison life can be improved. Additionally, imprisonment can be and is becoming more of a punishment of last resort than it has been in the recent past. There is increasing awareness of the need for reform and revitalization of probation (even though there is a countercurrent toward abolition of probation). Alternative sentencing to community service or restitution programs in which the offender works to repay the victim of a property crime may decrease the need for prison sentences. But, given the range and quantity of crime in the United States and the political popularity of stern remedies, it would be unrealistic to expect the nearby demise of the prison system.[5]

Whereas the problems of imprisonment attract comparatively little public attention, capital punishment is often in the headlines. Most of the widely reported Supreme Court argument and decision has concerned the question of whether capital punishment is "cruel and unusual." In 1976 in *Gregg v. Georgia* and allied cases, the Court decided that capital punishment is not cruel and unusual per se and is constitutionally permissible under certain conditions. Accordingly, capital punishment resumed in 1977. It should be apparent that moral issues underly the constitutional ones. If punishment is cruel, there is reason to reject it. If it is unusual, it will not likely be fair. While retributivists for the most part agree with Immanuel Kant that execution is sometimes morally acceptable or even required, utilitarians disagree among themselves on the justifiability of capital punishment. This is largely because they are uncertain about the deterrent value of the prospect of death, while they are as aware as anyone of the severity of that punishment. The argument that capital punishment is necessary as the capstone of a deterrent system of legal threats is, at present, a standoff between opponents and advocates of that penalty. In general, it is difficult, if not impossible, to show that there is any significant difference in homicide rates between states that execute and sociologically similar states that do not.

Just as with the general practice of legal punishment, imprisonment and capital punishment must be shown to have defensible purposes and to operate within morally acceptable boundaries. If neither of these practices served any deterrent purpose, then it would be difficult to defend them on moral grounds because they would then inflict merely gratuitous suffering or death. If they are not administered fairly and with respect for the persons who fall under them (a respect due to persons as persons, even to felons), then they violate the moral boundaries of acceptability. The most serious question about capital punishment (aside from the possibility of uncorrectable injustice to an innocent) has no parallel in consideration of imprisonment. It is whether, even if it is administered in a perfectly evenhanded way under fair laws and is in this sense not cruel or unusual, it does not per se violate the principle that we should accord respect to each individual. Can we at once treat an individual with respect and take his life?

There are two problems about fines, as there are about imprisonment and capital punishment. Are they effective in discouraging crime? Are they morally acceptable means of discouragement? The relative economy of fines compared to imprisonment and capital punishment suggests that it might be advisable to experiment with more sophisticated systems of fining than have been used in the past. Let us assume, for the sake of this discussion, that there is at least some deterrent effect in the prospect of a fine and that there is, by and large, greater deterrent effect in more severe fines. The latter assumption would be subject, in a more detailed discussion, to a number of qualifications, some of which we notice next.

A problem peculiar to fines, but not to imprisonment and capital punishment, concerns the punitive nature of a fine. There is ordinarily little question that a person imprisoned or hanged is punished; but does it follow that because I have paid a fine for overparking I have been punished? Or suppose that a court requires me to make triple restitution to a person whom I have defrauded? This is certainly more like punishment, yet it is also not a little like the settlement of a civil suit. But if I am fined what is for me a large sum because I have littered a public park, this pretty clearly falls under the heading of punishment. In any case, there should be no problem in principle in fitting a great many cases of fining under the general definition of punishment in Chapter 1. The questionable cases have largely to do with the intent of the fining. Is it really or primarily the fulfillment of a threat that should a person engage in a forbidden practice she will suffer in some way? Or is it a means of raising revenue or of satisfying claims of one party against another?

While the economy of fining may be a point in their favor, moral objections can arise over the apparent unfairness of that mode of punishment. It seems a system ready-made to favor the rich over the poor. If Croesus pays a $200 fine for littering, he may hardly notice the increase in his daily cash expenditures, whereas Villon may have to go hungry for a month. This objection may be not so much against fining, however, as against fixed fines. If the fine for littering were a day's income (not only pay), Croesus might in the future be as careful as Villon about tossing his beer can on the highway. Fining so many day's income may still be morally questionable if the person fined is living on the margin of poverty. A morally aware system would probably have to instruct judges to take into account the economic circumstances and family responsibilities of the offender. It is worth noting that while rather sophisticated systems of "day fines" (as opposed to fixed "tariffs" for given crime categories) are in use in Scandinavia and Germany, fines as punishment have received relatively little attention in the United States.

Moral concerns would no doubt mount if fines were instituted for the more serious crimes, those that result in bodily injury, suffering, or death. The problem here would be that a potential assaulter or murderer could, in theory, calculate what it would be worth to her to go through with her crime and that, whatever the fine, she might be better off than her injured or dead victim. A system that allowed or encouraged such calculations would be morally repugnant. In civil proceedings that seem morally acceptable, a decision may require payment for injury, but the public posting of a "price list" for injuries seems barbarous.[6] But it is unclear how fines could serve to deter in the absence of at least an indication of what the fine would be for a crime.

The assumption of arguments of this sort against fines as punishment may be that fines are relatively painless and that punishment should be painful. But given a world in which money is the universal medium of exchange and in which, in consequence, to deprive a person of money is to deprive him of some portion of what he can buy with that money, it would seem that he can suffer a meaningful loss. At the least, it seems that more thought and experiment might be given to forms of fining that are keyed to the income of the person paying the fine. This is to recognize that fining might, no matter how closely keyed, be harder on the very poorest persons and may not be applicable to them. But, then, to send the head of a poor family to jail is hard, too. It hardly needs mentioning, in favor of fining, that it is to be preferred on economic grounds to imprisonment, given the costs per day of imprisonment.

THREE ADDRESSEES OF JUSTIFICATION

It is useful, in thinking about the justification of a practice, to ask *to whom* the justification is addressed. Typically, it will be addressed to those persons or classes of persons particularly affected, as well as to the general public. Punishment is no exception. The addressees we should bear in mind are the victim, the criminal, and the public.

We must show the victim that the punishment response is one that makes clear that she cannot be injured with impunity, that her injury *matters*, that the community is concerned about her injury at the hands of the criminal. That is to say, that what is paramount is respect—respect for the victim as a person exhibited in the way that society deals with the offender. If the community's concern is merely to reduce crime, by whomever committed on whatever victim, the particular victim of crime might rightly suspect that the injury he suffers does not much matter. To justify punishment to the victims, it will not do therefore to speak only of deterrence.

Justifying the punishment to the *criminal* is, as we have seen in our discussion of retributivism, a complex matter. Respect requires that we not use the criminal as a mere means to promote some end, even if the end we have in mind is the well-being of society as a whole. If this were the sole consideration, then the punishment-of-the-innocent argument would be devastatingly relevant. Here the reference to what the criminal deserves seems germane—provided that a meaningful account can be given of how desert may be decided.

The *public's* major concern is protection: that it be shielded from crime. What the public must be shown is that the practice of punishment is necessary to prevent the harms that crime causes: injury, death, loss of property, indignity, suffering. It must be shown that the practice of punishment is an appropriate manifestation of concern for the well-being of everyone. Only when punishment is instituted in response to this concern do questions of respect and fairness arise. Only if cosmic desert is presupposed may we say that the purpose of punishment is that justice be done. But, given the practice of punishment, justice must be done if the practice is to work in a morally justifiable way. It would seem strange to say that the practice of punishment is instituted out of respect for either the victim or the criminal. But the practice of punishment, once in force, is constrained by the moral requirement of respect for both.

CONCLUSION

It was apparent at the end of the last chapter that we needed a new beginning if we were to make moral sense of legal punishment. The approach we used in this chapter was to consider legal punishment as one among several alternative practices designed to meet a social need, the need to ensure compliance with a working set of rules. Social reform, treatment, persuasion, and genetic analysis were mentioned as alternatives. No one of these practices is found morally defensible as a substitute for punishment, although each or all of them could be complementary to that practice. If all of this is accepted, punishment is not eliminable as a morally justifiable practice, and there are positive reasons to prefer it when it is considered as a reverse-pricing system.

But punishment as a practice can be justified only if there are morally justifiable methods of punishment. We examined imprisonment and capital punishment from this point of view. We concluded that punishment could not be justified if the only available modes of punishment were imprisonment and execution, as those practices function at present in the United States. But we recognized in passing that there are more options for punishment than these two, including especially a more sophisticated system of fines.

We closed by noting the importance of remembering the addressee of justification because different sorts of consideration might be necessary to meet the expectations of differently situated addressees. With respect to the practice of punishment, we mentioned the peculiar relevance of considerations of respect to the victim, of fairness to the criminal, and of beneficence to the public. Because all these parties are necessarily involved in crime (unless there are "victimless crimes"), it should not be surprising that the respective types of consideration are relevant to the justification of punishment.

But we must now turn to a looming problem, one that may well have been troubling the reader. How can punishment be justified if no one is or few people are responsible for their crimes? If this were so, what defensible purpose could punishment serve? And in the absence of defensible purpose, would not punishment be morally wrong?

NOTES

1. The reconciliation would presuppose an undifferentiated consequential-
    ism, thus bracketing for the time being the question of what kinds of con-
    sequence are to have sole relevance.

2. As we have noticed, utilitarianism as a theory of ethics is broader than this.
    But, applied to the problem of criminal behavior, the theory may be read
    in this way, provided we remember that the utilitarian has no particular
    affection for punishment. It is for him simply one practice among others
    that may be useful for the purpose of minimizing crime.

3. Crime might on this ground be distinguished from mere wrongdoing.
    Consider the teacher who must deal with the child who insists that there
    had been no rule against pouring glue in the classroom seats.

4. *New York Times*, 18 Dec. 1985. Skeptics have been quick to point out that
    such programs may be subject to abuses and that the recidivism rates of
    graduates have been about the same as those of state penitentiaries. How-
    ever, the program may be successful in deterring nonviolent young men
    for whom crime has not yet become a hardened way of life (*Time*, 16 Oct.
    1989, pp. 17–18).

5. For a sophisticated discussion of the limited deterrent value of imprison-
    ment, see Gottfredson and Hirschi, passim.

6. While it may seem morally offensive to moderns, it should be noted that
    such a list was a feature of many ancient codes from the Old Testament to
    the Edicts of Asoka. If a judgment on the morality of those codes is possi-
    ble at all, it would certainly have to be based on a full understanding of the
    circumstances in which the codes were published.

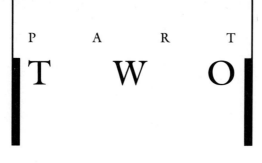

P A R T

T W O

Responsibility

CHAPTER 4

Skepticism About Responsibility

It will be useful to bear in mind as we survey some of the sources of suspicion concerning personal responsibility that the target of the skeptic is not always well-defined, nor is it necessarily clear what the defender of responsibility is defending. I will try to delineate in Chapter 5 what I, at least, am defending. I assume that what is to be defended is a practice, and in Chapter 5, I will try to specify what practice or set of practices is in question.

No practice under which people are held liable for their deeds can be morally justifiable if people can't help doing what they do. That is the force of the deterministic position of whatever variety. In this chapter, we examine some of those varieties. As we do so, it would be well to bear in mind that determinism can be more or less extreme. The most extreme form amounts to this:

1. No one can help doing what they do.

2. No one is responsible for what they can't help doing.

3. Hence, no one is responsible.

Less extreme determinists deny universal scope to (1) or argue that (2) does not necessarily follow. Less extreme determinists may therefore endorse a practice whereby persons are held responsible, but they may have reservations about the range of that practice because they may believe that relatively few people can help doing what they do.

The deterministic position can take different forms depending on the support that is offered for the proposition that no one can help doing what they do. The support offered may be scientific (or pseudoscientific) or metaphysical. We will discuss these varieties of determinism.

There are also nondeterminist skeptics: practical, technological, and moral ones. Practical skeptics hold that it is just not worthwhile to go into questions of responsibility, that to do so makes ineffective legal systems. Technological skeptics contend that what is paramount is social control and that efficient social control bypasses all questions of responsibility. Moral skeptics think it wrong, inconsistent with an enlightened morality, to insist on individual responsibility for harm. We will examine these nondeterminist skeptical positions after a look at some varieties of scientific skepticism and at metaphysical skepticism concerning personal responsibility.

"SCIENTIFIC" SKEPTICISM

The general form of "scientific" skepticism argues that it can be scientifically established that human beings are unable to control their propensity for crime. Forces beyond the possibility of individual control determine the way people behave.

The anthropologist Melville Herskovits argues, for example, that "judgments are based on experience and experience is interpreted by each individual in terms of his own enculturation" (Herskovits, p. 631). Enculturation, in turn, takes place early in life. The child has no choice whether or how to be encultured; she is simply the creature, the creation, of her culture. Because enculturation determines how she will behave, it would be mistaken to attribute that behavior to the person's own will. It is not the person but the culture that is responsible. If enculturation determines that strangers can be killed at will, that females can be enslaved, or that forests can be burned to make room for agriculture, it is useless to argue that the individual who engages in these practices is a wrongdoer because that implies that the individual could do right. But "wrong" and "right" can only be understood by reference to that person's enculturation and by the hypothesis that is the way she is encultured.

Supposing that there is such a thing as "Western culture," it might seem as if culturally relativistic skepticism were not very damaging to the thesis that persons may be justifiably held responsible for their deeds. If most of us share the same culture, then how does Herskovits's relativism prevent you from holding me responsible for violating some norm of our shared culture — for injuring a third person, say?

The difficulty is that once the notion of enculturation is introduced, the conclusion that there is a distinct enculturation process for each individual in the population seems unavoidable. Ruth Benedict recognizes separate cultures within what might formerly have been held to be one culture. There is, for example, the culture of the working class and of the white-collar class. There is also a culture unique to each generation within the separate classes. The grandson's culture is not identical with that of the grandfather. Edward Sapir carries this reasoning to the logical conclusion by asserting that each person is the bearer of a unique and personal culture. Given different factors in each person's enculturation, it is not reasonable to suppose that any person's enculturation is identical with the enculturation of any other. Even children in the same relatively stable family will be differently encultured because they come along at different times in the family history. The experience of the youngest child will be different from that of the oldest, for example. The family fortunes may be better or worse, the parents will be older, the community will have changed, and he will have older siblings.

If all of this were granted, then the thesis of cultural relativism would indeed be damaging to the assumption that persons are individually responsible for their deeds. The argument against that assumption becomes more pointed, indeed poignant, when it is shown that in nontribal societies enculturation can be planned and implemented—and that this very intentional enculturation may be responsible for the individual's behavior. The force of this argument was recognized by Robert Owen, a nineteenth-century British social reformer whom we have met in Chapter 2. He contended, based on his experience as a mill manager in Scotland, that the very people—the owners and stockholders, the gentry and clergy—who shaped the enculturation of mill workers as children were then ready to imprison them for the crimes that, given their enculturation, they were bound to commit. By reducing working hours, providing day-care facilities, ceasing to employ small children in the mills, and building decent homes for workers, Owen succeeded in reducing crime (Owen, 1816, p. 14).

A number of claims have been made—some of them worthy of attention, some not—that crime is to greater or less degree the result of genetic inheritance. In the nineteenth century, the Italian criminologists Garofalo, Ferri, and Lombroso argued that it was possible to pick out criminals from the general population by inherited characteristics like low brows and cauliflower ears. In this century, the presence of the XYY chromosome has been held to characterize criminals.

E. O. Wilson and other "sociobiologists" have developed a more sophisticated form of the genetically deterministic argument. They hold that the biological characteristics that determine our responses are themselves determined by the process of natural selection. Says Wilson,

> The biologist, who is concerned with . . . physiology and evolutionary history, realizes that self-knowledge is constrained and shaped by the emotional control centers in the hypothalamus and limbic systems of the brain. These centers flood our consciousness with all the emotions—hate, love, guilt, fear, and others—that are consulted by ethical philosophers who wish to intuit the standards of good and evil. What, we are then compelled to ask, made the hypothalamus and limbic system? They evolved by natural selection. . . . (p. 3)

If natural selection then accounts for our emotions and if emotions cause our actions, responsibility must rest on natural selection for the good and evil things that we do.

In the first half of this century, many psychiatrists and psychologists held that crime is best understood as a symptom of disease. For example, Benjamin Karpman told us that

> criminal behavior is an unconsciously conditional psychic reaction over which [criminals] have no conscious control. . . . We have to treat them as psychically sick people which in every respect they are. It is no more reasonable to punish these individuals . . . than it is to punish an individual for breathing through his mouth because of enlarged adenoids, when a simple operation will do the trick. (p. 584)

Gregory Zilboorg went further, insisting that, given that criminal behavior is beyond control, the urge to punish criminals is itself a pathological condition:

> Our anxiety can be quieted down only in one of two ways: In our sudden unconscious denial of any similarity with the criminal we can hurl ourselves upon him with all the power of our aggressive, punitive, destructive hostility; or we can assume the criminal to be a mentally sick man and can then assume a more tolerant or charitable attitude toward the doer if not the deed. (p. 80)

While such extreme statements are rare today, there is still a good deal of tension between the psychiatric and legal communities over the nature of criminal behavior. It is, from the medical point of view, something that signals a condition that needs curing; from the point of view of the law, it is behavior that warrants control.

METAPHYSICAL SKEPTICISM

The deterministic metaphysical argument turns on the claims that all events are necessitated by their causes and that, given their causes, they could not be otherwise. Those events that are human actions follow necessarily from a nexus of causes extending back through history and beyond. Thus, no agent can justifiably be held responsible for her action. The responsibility lies with the causes of her action. This is (except for theological metaphysics) no more than the generalization of scientific skepticism. Whether the causes in question are cultural, psychological, physiological, psychiatric, or genetic, responsibility slides off of the agent and back onto the causes. What the metaphysical formulation of the argument makes explicit is a premise that is only implicit in scientific skepticism: the claim that causes *necessitate* their consequences. Given the causes, the consequences, including wrong action, could not have been otherwise than what they were. If the action was necessitated, then the agent could not help having done it. If she could not have helped doing it, she can't be responsible for it.

What kind of necessity is this? If it is to serve the purpose of the argument, it must be a kind of coercive necessity, such as the necessity that I fall from a cliff if I am pushed over the edge. Critics of metaphysical determinism question this interpretation of causation. It assumes that if one event is caused by another, it is somehow coerced by the other event. But causation is better understood, it is argued, as regularity: Events of one type regularly follow events of another type.

This traditional (if not hoary) metaphysical position is countered by an equally traditional one. Advocates of free will deny that *all* events are necessitated by anterior causes. "Acts of will" (from which actions follow) are freely made. It has been argued, however, that this attempt to rescue individual responsibility fails because a completely uncaused act of will is independent of the formed character of the agent and is therefore not properly attributable to him. Be all of this as it may, it would be inappropriate and unwise to do more than mention these positions here, noting that not only the metaphysically deterministic position but also the freewill theory are held to be inconsistent with the ascription of personal responsibility.

PRACTICAL SKEPTICISM

The sort of skepticism I have labeled as "practical" amounts to this: (1) It is difficult and time-consuming as a matter of practice to determine whether a person could have helped doing what she did—to determine, for example, whether she was suffering from some mental disability at the time of the act or to decide whether the behavior was really intentional. (2) Therefore, as a matter of legal practice, we should bypass such enquiries and assess liability for acts done without regard to "real" or "true" responsibility.

The best-known advocate of such a "strict liability" position is Baroness Barbara Wootton. Wootton begins from a straightforward utilitarian position. The business of the criminal courts is to prevent crime, not to punish wickedness. Crime can be prevented more effectively if the court is spared the time and effort of determining the presence or absence of *mens rea* (guilty mind) at the time that the *actus reus* (the forbidden act) was committed. . . . [T]he material consequences of an action, and the reasons for prohibiting it, are the same whether it is the result of sinister malicious plotting, or negligence or of sheer accident. . . . (Feinberg and Gross, 546)

The concept of responsibility, says Wootton, "should be allowed to wither away" as strict liability fills its place. This applies to all the defenses a person may marshal to show that, although he may have committed an act that is prohibited, nevertheless he should not be declared guilty. Mental incapacity in the form of weak-mindedness or insanity are among the defenses not to be allowed. They are to be excluded as defenses, even though there may be utilitarian reasons for taking them into account after "conviction." "[M]ens rea," Wootton contends, "has . . . *got into the wrong place*. . . ." What motivated the law-breaker or whether he suffered from mental deficiency should not be considered at the stage of what is presently called conviction. The law could have been violated by a person who is careless, wicked, or mentally deficient. Or it could have been a merely unfortunate and unavoidable accident. Those are matters to be sorted out in determining what sort of treatment, if any, is needed.

After conviction, the court may apply compulsory measures (penal or therapeutic) in the "most appropriate way from the point of view of society." Properly speaking, from Wootton's perspective one would not punish at all. If, in the last resort, a person does not respond to therapy, she may be detained in a place of safekeeping for the benefit of society. But such detainment should not be confused with punishment.

H. L. A. Hart (1968, pp. 193–209; Feinberg and Gross, 561–567) responds to this proposal by arguing that there are some crimes—for example, attempts—that by their very nature require an inquiry into *mens rea*, that the freedom of the individual to choose whether to violate the law is invaded and that it is morally wrong to treat purported offenders as mere means to the supposed good of society.

Wootton would, on slightly deeper analysis, have difficulty maintaining her thesis, even granted the utilitarian assumption from which it begins. From the utilitarian point of view, it should be a purpose of the criminal law to make possible or likely the socialization of those who fall under the law. We will therefore, as good utilitarians, not encourage those who take advantage over others by violating the law. But if no defenses are allowed, given the overt act done, then no distinction is possible between the person who has developed the requisite socially desirable dispositions and the person who has not—between the person who takes advantage and the person who has made a mistake or who is not mentally normal. The court will regard them equally as candidates for whatever disposition is socially advantageous. There is nothing socially beneficial in such a procedure. What is neglected by Wootton in the name of utilitarian advantage is the role of the law in the development of a rule-abiding citizenry.

TECHNOLOGICAL SKEPTICISM

B. F. Skinner argues that

1. The control of behavior is socially necessary, since humans, unlike ants, do not behave in an orderly way by instinct.

2. The purpose of responsibility–ascription is to control behavior.

3. There are more efficient means of controlling behavior than the use of such a practice. Early positive reinforcement, for example, makes us want to do what the controller wants us to do. Hence we do not resist control.

4. We should not use inefficient means of control when efficient means are readily available.

5. Hence, we should abandon the practice of ascribing responsibility. (Chs. 2 and 3)

In a characteristic passage, Skinner tells us that

> [a]ll these questions about purposes, feelings, knowledge, and so on, can be restated in terms of the environment to which a person has been exposed. What a person "intends to do" depends upon what he has done in the past and what has then happened. . . . Whether he deserves punishment when all these conditions are taken into account is a question about probable results: will he, if punished, behave in a different way when similar circumstances again arise? There is a current tendency [of which Skinner approves] to substitute controllability for responsibility, and controllability . . . explicitly alludes to external conditions. (p. 72)

MORAL SKEPTICISM

Jesus, as is well known, taught that passing judgment on other persons for what they have done is at best questionable and at worst morally wrong. That is, anyway, a common modern interpretation of the "mote and beam" passage and of the admonition "let him who is without sin cast the first stone." Whether or not Jesus is correctly interpreted, there is quite certainly a contemporary sense that one must have moral standing to judge the actions of other people and that most of us most of the time do not have that standing. One of the worst things one can do, we believe, is to anoint oneself as a scourge of wrongdoing, a pillar of righteousness, or a censor of backsliders. It is bad because it reveals something about ourselves: We assume the mantle of God—place ourselves in the seat of judgment, a seat where as mere humans we have no right to be. "'Judgment is mine' saith the Lord."

This reticence, the sense that we should leave judgment to God, is reinforced by modern discoveries of the intricacies of the human mind, of mind as the great trickster, deceiving even ourselves in judgment of our own motives and intentions. We can't from mere externals know the motivations, the inner workings of the psyche, that led another to do what he did. I will suggest in Chapter 5 that the question of whether we are morally entitled to hold another responsible is a confused one, that it confuses what I call Compensation Responsibility with Blame Responsibility.

THE SHRINKING CIRCLE OF RESPONSIBILITY

In the twentieth century, personal responsibility for harm has diminished. There are many reasons for this trend. I will mention a few of them: some good and some not so good.

First, it has become increasingly apparent that losses incurred in such ordinary and necessary occupations as driving an automobile to work, treating patients, or calculating a client's taxes had better not be allowed to fall suddenly and catastrophically on the person who brings about the loss. In consequence, schemes for insurance and reinsurance tend to spread such losses across many people — the people who enter into a scheme by buying liability insurance. Individuals are also less likely to suffer the consequences of their prodigality or bad judgment because, through government-mandated self-insurance — Social Security — they will be provided for (minimally) in their old age. Workmen's compensation, also government-mandated, places the employer differently and more distantly in the network of claims for injury. Most interesting, for present purposes, is the spread of no-fault insurance. This is a subject that we will consider, in its more general implications, in Chapter 7. No-fault insurance involves the abandonment of attempts to determine who is at fault in automobile accidents and the settlement of the loss by the insurers of the persons involved.

Second, there is the trend, applauded by Wootton and others, toward the spread of strict liability in law. To say that a person is strictly liable for an offense is to say that none of the ordinarily applicable defenses apply. For example, she cannot plead mistake, inadvertence, or accident. This might seem a trend toward an enlargement of the circle of personal responsibility, but it in fact works in the opposite direction. To put the point briefly, the person who brings about the harm is held liable without regard to her personal responsibility. We would ordinarily say that a person who did something by accident was not responsible for the harm she caused, provided, of course, that she was exercising reasonable care. Thus, for strict liability offenses, personal responsibility is explicitly set aside, made irrelevant.

Strict liability in law is, of course, no newcomer. It has long been a doctrine that ignorance of the law is no excuse. Generally speaking, the vendor of alcoholic beverages to a minor or of mislabeled food, adulterated drugs, or contaminated milk to the general public is liable no matter what precautions he may have taken to avoid violating the law. The man who has intercourse with a consenting woman, and who has good reasons to think that she is over the legally prescribed age of consent, may still be guilty of statutory rape if she is not. The woman who marries for a second time, in the well-founded belief that her first husband is dead, may still be guilty of bigamy.

Third, personal responsibility shrinks because the pool of persons eligible to be held responsible diminishes with the expansion of the categories of the noneligible. Juveniles are either exempt from criminal proceedings or are accorded special treatment in a juvenile court and in juvenile detention or reformatory institutions. With greater understanding of the nature and causes of mental deficiencies, an increasing percentage of the population is recognized as deficient and hence as not eligible to be held liable for the harm they have caused.

Underlying the tendency to expand the limits of mental deficiency is a deeper trend toward the acceptance of *explanation* of a person's behavior as *justification* of that behavior. If the behavior can be understood, assigned natural or social causes, then it is, if not morally acceptable, at least morally neutral — not a proper object of blame or punishment.

Fourth, the sphere of personal responsibility shrinks because of the increased availability of sophisticated drugs and methods of behavior modification (see the earlier remarks on Skinner). Given this greatly augmented capacity to control human behavior, the assignment of personal responsibility can seem little more than a comparatively inefficient means of behavior control. Whether this is an appropriate perspective on the practice of ascribing responsibility is questionable.

Finally, personal responsibility is increasingly diffused through collectivities like corporations and government institutions. The greater the complexity of the organization, the more difficult it is to speak meaningfully of the responsibility of any person within it for the harm that the organization may have caused. Was Lieutenant Calley responsible for the massacre at My Lai, for example, or was the responsibility elsewhere in the chain of command; or was it simply that no given individual can be held responsible, given the structure of command? (French)

CONCLUSION

We have distinguished different forms of skepticism concerning responsibility and have found some of the reasons for the diminishing concern with personal responsibility. But what, more exactly, is the target of these skeptical doubts? I suggest that it is a practice or a set of practices. When can we properly say, under that practice, or those practices, that a person *is responsible*? Until we have a clearer picture of that which is under attack, we are unlikely to arrive at any very judicious analysis of its merits and demerits. It is to the sketching of that picture that we now turn.

CHAPTER 5

Ascribing Responsibility

Skepticism about responsibility is both widespread and differently motivated. It is difficult to be sure just what is its target. What are the skeptics being skeptical about? In this chapter, I suggest that to raise a doubt about whether anyone is responsible, intentionally or not, is to question a social practice or practices. Speaking of a person as "responsible" is intelligible only given the context of the practices of responsibility–ascription. *Responsible* is a term more like *checkmate* than like *yellow* or *soft*. *Checkmate* is intelligible only given the practice of chess playing. *Yellow* and *soft* are not in that way practice-dependent for their meaning. To understand *responsible*, it is necessary to understand the related practices that lend meaning to the term, to grasp the way in which to be responsible is to fall into a role determined by the rules of the practices.

If responsibility–ascription were merely a practice for determining who is to wear a certain label, there would be nothing to justify. The practice would be as practically and morally neutral as chess. What matters is what is assumed to follow from the pinning on of the label—a response of some kind. What needs justification are practices in which there will be particular kinds of response to the person so labeled. The response might be blame, legal punishment, or the requirement that a person make good a loss. For convenience, I speak of Liability Responsibility as the practice by which we determine who wears the label. As the responses of blame, punishment, or the requirement that compensation be made are added, I speak of Blame Responsibility, Punishment Responsibility, and Compensation Responsibility. My first move therefore is to depict as clearly as I can the keystone to an understanding of the family of responsibility–ascription practices: Liability Responsibility.

LIABILITY RESPONSIBILITY

What is it to "hold someone liable"? The answer is more complicated than it might at first seem, and tracing out even a broad and preliminary answer requires that we bring on stage some central concepts of the philosophy of law. Let us start with a bare-bones example, details to be filled in as we go along. Able says to Baker, "You are responsible for the loss of the battle."

What is going on here? There is a kind of finger pointing, a picking-out of Baker from other persons who were on the losing side of the battle. The loss of the battle is *imputed to* Baker. The imputation can be formal, involving administrators, prosecutors, judges, juries, and due process of law. Or it can be informal, where the finger pointer is a witness, acquaintance, friend, or enemy. It can be a declaration pronounced by someone, a general or a judge, in authority; or it can be just an accusation that may eventually lead to such a declaration.

Able, the *imputer*, may be a person acting on his own or he may be acting as a member, representative, or official of some group, organization, or government. He may even be (if we are to keep our sketch of the practice as wide as possible) the representative, or agent, of a personlike being or beings: a priest, seer, or prophet.

Baker, the *imputee*, may be a person, a group of persons, a personlike being (gods, spirits), even an animal or a material object.

The loss of the battle is a stand-in for a *harm* of some kind, and there can be many kinds of harm: death, injury, pain, interference, damage, destruction, frustration, reduction of value, misery, thwarted plans. (There can be liability for good consequences, too—"Who is responsible for the happy atmosphere in this office?"—but law tends to focus on harms.) Harms may or may not be compensable or restitutable. Harms may be near or remote in time. They may come about through chains of human agency or be relatively direct, the immediate result of what Baker has done or failed to do. Baker may be simply an inattentive sentry or he may lead the division that failed to take an enemy stronghold.

If Able wants to make good his accusation, he must point to something that Baker *did or failed to do*, to Baker's negligence or recklessness, or perhaps to the acts or failures to act of those who are in some way under Baker's authority. Baker slept on duty or he failed to muster enough firepower to break through the enemy line.

Baker's misdeeds or failures may be understood against the background of *the requirements of the role(s)* that Baker was playing. These roles may be institutional or situational. Soldier, general, judge, teacher, reporter, or fire fighter are institutional roles. To understand them, it is necessary to understand the practices that together constitute the institution, including other roles that are played according to the rules of those practices. Thus, we cannot understand the role of general without some understanding of what an army is and what it is supposed to accomplish. A situational role is one into which anyone may fall, not as a result of having a role in an institution. Thus, Baker might have brought about some harm or failed to avert one in his role as bungling rescuer, imprecise witness of a crime, or inattentive pedestrian. Institutional or situational roles may be entered into voluntarily or involuntarily. Thus, a person may be a reporter by choice, but a soldier as a result of the draft. Or one may be a passerby by chance, but a rescuer by choice.

Baker may, conceding that a harm was brought about by something he did or did not do, still offer reasons why he is not responsible for the harm in question, or not fully responsible. He may claim immunity or incapacity; or he may offer an excuse or a justification. In Chapter 6, we will consider the *defenses* that fall under these general headings.

THE BOUNDARIES
OF RESPONSIBILITY–ASCRIPTION

This sketch is broad enough to cover nearly any liability–ascribing practice that may be in question in skeptical attacks. What is to count as a practice of Liability Responsibility is inevitably a matter for judgment. Generally, to whatever extent the previously mentioned requirements fall off, to that extent the practice in question has less claim to be one of liability–ascription. Could we still be engaged in that practice if, for example, there were no imputer, or no imputee, or no harm (or good consequence)? It seems unlikely that we would be willing to call any such practices liability–ascription practices. On the other hand, we may, as is apparent soon, still have such a practice if a harm can be imputed to Baker in the absence of any act on Baker's part or (given an act) in the absence of any causal relation between Baker's act and the harm for which he is held responsible.

What is at issue in these speculations is not which versions of liability–ascription are morally acceptable but which practices are to count as examples of liability–ascription.

The sketch is accommodating enough to cover a variety of historical practices that figure in the development of Anglo-American law. Under Roman law, for example, a private citizen could bring charges and prosecute for an offense that would now be a crime. If he did not prove his case, however, he was guilty of calumny and must suffer the consequences. This is a practice covered by our sketch because Able is widely enough defined. In early English criminal law, there was the institution of the frank-pledge according to which the citizens assigned to a group were responsible for the crimes of any member of that group. Again, the history of the English law of homicide traces the transition from a practice in which there is a right on the part of survivors to slay a slayer of their relative to a practice in which only the state has a right to kill a murderer. The account we have given does not specify who has a right to prosecute or to carry out a verdict. Also, in early English law, there is a transition from indifference to excuses that can be offered for homicide, to acceptance of the excuse of self-defense (Stephen, Ch. 26). But the sketch offered does not require that there should be excuses, only that such excuses as are recognized should be taken into account. Finally, in early English law (under the law of *deodands*), an inanimate object or an animal could be held liable under law to punishment for its crime. Thus, the beam that falls on a woman or the horse that kicks her may be appropriately punished for the woman's death. Deodand can be accommodated within the broad skirts of our sketch.

Our interest here is in personal liability. That may be defined as a practice in which Baker is a person or persons. He is not, as in the long history of the practice he might have been, a material thing, an animal, a god, an evil spirit, chance, or fate.

FURTHER REMARKS ON LIABILITY RESPONSIBILITY

It may be useful before we go further to set off Liability Responsibility from some related sorts of responsibility that are *not* the subject of discussion (Hart, 1968, 212 ff.).

The first sort, already mentioned, is *role responsibility*—the responsibility that one do what anyone playing a given role is properly expected to do: the police officer's responsibility to enforce the law, the attorney's responsibility to defend her client, the parent's responsibility for the education of his child, the driver's responsibility to pay attention to traffic signals.

Sometimes we say that X was responsible for Y, meaning merely that X caused Y: The meeting of warm, moist air from the gulf with cool air from the north was responsible for the rainstorm. A person may bear *causal responsibility* for a harm, even though she has a perfectly adequate defense and is thus not liability-responsible. She did bump into the teetering tourist on the edge of the Grand Canyon, but she was herself pushed by a running child.

On occasion, we speak of the degree to which a person is up to a certain mark, whether he is sane, mentally normal, or adult, for example. Here we have in mind *capacity responsibility*. Does the person have the requisite capacity under law, or in commonsense judgments, to be held responsible for having burned his boarding house to the ground?

We should add *overall responsibility* because it sometimes appears in discussions of responsibility. We sometimes commend a person as being responsible, meaning that she assumes responsibilities well—does not fail to carry through on commitments, recognizes that she is the person who should do what needs doing and does not leave it to others, or may be trusted to perform well in the role she has chosen.

Our topic, to this point, has been *Liability Responsibility*. It is (with important exceptions) a necessary condition of a person's being liable that he be capacity-responsible. It is a necessary condition that he be role-responsible. It is, with additional important exceptions, a necessary condition that he be causally responsible. Persons defending themselves against ascriptions of Liability Responsibility may plead that causal responsibility, role responsibility, or capacity responsibility was absent. They also may, granting liability, plead mitigation on the ground that their overall responsibility is excellent and that what they have done is uncharacteristic.

Liability typically turns on questions of contributory fault. The civil law makes this explicit. A person is contributorily at fault, in a case of negligent loss, if and only if she made a causal contribution to the loss, her conduct was faulty, and her faulty conduct resulted in the loss. It won't do if there is faulty conduct that is causally irrelevant to the loss incurred (Feinberg, 1970, p. 222). If, while running naked in the streets, she slips and breaks tables and chairs of a sidewalk café, her fault in running naked is not appropriately related to the loss of the tables and chairs. In the context of civil law, faulty conduct typically means conduct that violates a legal prohibition or requirement; or it means conduct that was negligent or reckless by the "reasonable man" standard — would not have been done or omitted by a reasonable man. The legally relevant fault of the naked runner was in negligently failing to look where she was going.

Given this understanding of contributory fault and of response, we can now look back to strict liability and define it as any liability for which the contributory fault condition is weakened or absent (Feinberg, 1970, p. 223).

Suppose then that a person is prima facie liability-responsible for a loss. He was at the wheel when his car plowed into his neighbor's living room. There is no question but that his driving the car contributed to the loss. He is then, both legally and morally, answerable. That is to say, he has an obligation, legal and moral, either to offer a defense or to accept liability. In the absence of a defense, he is open to the appropriate legal or moral responses if he is in fact liable. To say he is liable is to say that he was prima facie liable and that he offered no defense. It won't do to say that he had a defense but that he offered none . . . unless. Unless, that is, he has an appropriate defense for offering no defense!

| VARIETIES OF PERSONAL RESPONSIBILITY

There are a great many modes within which liability can be ascribed to persons. It will be useful, in understanding this point, to glance at some of them. As we have seen already, there can be formal or informal ways of ascribing responsibility, involving courts and boards on the one hand and the relations of parents, neighbors, and passersby on the other.

This suggests that we might classify liability–ascriptions by reference to the ascriber. Liability can be ascribed by individuals or groups. If by groups, it is by the informal means of kangaroo courts and public ballyhoo or through courts and boards, with varying emphases on the protections of due process of law. Historically and cross culturally, liability–ascription can be thought to stem from supernatural as well as from natural beings. God or the gods can hold a person or persons responsible, as Zeus holds Odysseus responsible for gouging out the eye of his son, the Cyclops. The ascriber can be the equal of the ascribee, or not the equal, under law and in the "moral court." In a democracy, whose laws incorporate no class distinctions, it theoretically makes no difference to the validity of an ascription of liability what the rank is of the person doing the ascribing. In a non-democratic polity, the notion that all are equal before the law must be emended by saying that all those of a given class are equal and higher-class ascribers may have more latitude than lower-class ones. A serf may not have the right, in a court of law, to ascribe responsibility to nobility.

We can classify ascriptions of responsibility by the route through which the ascription comes to the person said to be liable. While the paradigm case may be one in which one individual holds another liable for injury or damage, the reality of social life can lead us far from that paradigm. This distancing of ascription, through the complexities of social arrangement, can take place in two ways. First, the ascription of responsibility to someone may not be on account of the contributory fault of that particular person. It may, rather, be on account of the fault of some other person(s) for whose faults the ascribee is in some fashion responsible. The faulty action may have been done by a trigger-happy private whose too-early shots generated a fusillade that threw off General Baker's timing for his surprise attack. If an indicted defendant who has made bond skips to Brazil, the bondsman is responsible for making payment to the court. If a child bats a ball through a neighbor's window, the parent must make good the damage. Cases of this kind are sometimes labeled vicarious liability, the liability a person may suffer because of the acts or failures of another person or persons. But, second, ascription of liability may go down through a social network in such a way that no persons immediately involved in the loss are doing the ascribing or, at least, the formal ascribing, of Liability Responsibility. Thus, it is not up to the victims but to the prosecuting district attorney and the judge and jury to ascribe liability for the losses the victims suffer at the hands of a swindling stockbroker.

Assignments of Liability Responsibility to a given person may be arbitrary or nonarbitrary. An example of arbitrary assignment is the German practice, during World War II, of holding all members of a village responsible for the resistance of a small minority of inhabitants. The town of Lidice in Czechoslovakia was massacred as the result of such an assignment. The similarly motivated U.S. massacre at My Lai during the Vietnam War is another example. By saying that ascription of liability was arbitrary, I mean that no obligation was felt or honored that a link should be found between the activities of any particular member of the group massacred and the activities for which he or she was punished. To use the language introduced previously, there was no requirement of contributory fault.

This is true, as we have seen, of all assignments of strict liability, so that purely arbitrary ascriptions of liability are a subclass of strict liability. Although that subclass may not always be easy to distinguish from other subclasses of strict liability, what seems to set it off most clearly is the lack of any pretense that there need be contributory fault on the part of the person held liable. Strict liability legislation typically falls on persons who have voluntarily assumed the risk of liability by playing the particular role that they play: driver of a car, manager of a milk plant, or vendor of alcoholic beverages. She enters into a game in which the possible benefits outweigh the possible losses. By entering it, she accepts some version of the doctrine that, whatever the circumstances, "the buck stops" with her. Not so, unfortunately, the inhabitants, especially the children, of Lidice or My Lai. The conviction, under strict liability law, of a milk-plant manager whose product is polluted despite his most strenuous precautions need imply nothing about his fault and, in consequence, his blameworthiness. But the inhabitant of one of those unfortunate villages is held at fault while no obligation is felt to show where the fault lies. Perhaps the best way to summarize the difference between the two sorts of case is to say that, whereas arbitrary liability is a mere instrument of control, strict liability is typically not merely that but control for some identifiable and generally acceptable social end, such as wholesome food or safe highways.

HARM

If a wrongdoer is liable to a response, she must have done wrong either by doing or by failing to do something. (For simplicity, I speak of what *she* did or failed to do, even though we now recognize that her liability may be vicarious: may stem from what her servant, subordinate, ward, or agent may have done.) But also the wrong that she did must have contributed to some harm, or it must have been likely to contribute to harm. While her wrongdoing is a necessary condition of her liability, the liability is not for the wrongdoing but for the harm or likelihood of harm that results or might result from it. It is in virtue of the harm, including the likelihood of harm, that the wrongdoer is liable to a response appropriate to the harm.

To say that the wrongdoer may be liable for the harm *likely* to be caused is to say that, for example, he can also do wrong simply by running a red light, driving seventy in a thirty-miles-per-hour zone, or failing to have his car inspected. He can also, without violating such explicitly stated requirements or prohibitions, behave negligently or recklessly.

It can be argued, and has persuasively been argued (Feinberg, 1985, pp. 10–22), that legal responses are appropriate not only to harm but also on occasion to offense. If a passenger's behavior on a bus that people must ride to work is sufficiently disgusting, that behavior should be curbed by law. This contention relies on a finer distinction between offense and harm than I will attempt here. If a bus passenger's behavior is utterly repulsive and distracting, I say that the other passengers, unwilling spectators of that behavior, have suffered a harm. They cannot concentrate on their reading or their plans for the day; their appetites for breakfast, and perhaps for several other meals, are taken away; they are unable to enjoy the morning air and scenery on the way to work; and they dread repetitions of such experiences each time they board a bus.

ACT

An old jurisprudential saw is that "the requirement of an act is a cornerstone of our liberty." This is a confusing way of saying that a people cannot, if they are to remain free, be subject to punishment for what they have merely thought or discussed. They ought not, for example, be punished for their religious beliefs. They ought only be punished if they proceed to *do* something that is prohibited because doing it will or is likely to cause harm. This is, of course, wrong. A country in which there are thought police is not a free country. But because there are justifiable, positive legal requirements in a free society—such as the duty to register for the draft, to render aid to the victim of an accident, to watch where one is driving, to pay one's taxes, or to leash one's dog—it is justifiable to hold people liable for *not* acting when they should have acted. A glance at the list of crimes should easily persuade us that it is not only positive acts that constitute crimes. Consider, for example, possession of a forbidden substance, conspiracy (which requires only that one party act), or being an accessory by counseling the lawbreaker.

A deeper confusion turns around the question of how we are to distinguish an act from its consequences. It is notoriously difficult to say, in abstraction from any practical concern, where the act ends and the consequences begin. Suppose the engineer of a train pulls the emergency cord that brings the train to a halt, thereby causing the following train to plow into hers. What was the act, and what were the consequences? Was the act causing a wreck, stopping the train, pulling the emergency cord, grasping the emergency cord and moving her arm downward, placing her hand in a curved position on the emergency cord, flexing the muscles of her hand and arm, willing to flex her muscles, setting herself to will to flex her muscles, or, perhaps, setting herself to set herself to will to flex her muscles?

The philosophical motive of this curious line of questioning is worth trying to make clear. The thought is that we should hold people liability-responsible only for what they are *really* responsible for doing, for an *act* that is indisputably theirs. If we do not find such an act, then we may be holding a person liable for the consequences of an act. But he may not be liable for the consequences. He may not be really responsible for them. The farther we move out from acts of will (or of setting oneself to will), the greater the chance that there is some contingency, some reason why the person we hold liable is not really responsible. For example, the engineer might have stopped the train by accident if there was a faulty control, or she might have been thrown against the brake cord by a drunken stoker. Willing to do something does not in this way seem open to the contingencies that may qualify our judgment that the engineer is responsible. The willing is quite certainly her doing; the consequences may have been beyond her control.

Even though we have seen that wrongdoers may quite properly be held liable for *not* acting when they fail to do what is justifiably required of them, let us for the sake of argument suppose that it is only for acts that persons may justifiably be held liable. Would the metaphysical position be a defensible one that it is only for acts of will (or for settings, or settings to set) that a person may justifiably be held responsible because it is only those acts that are properly *his*? The question is puzzling because it presupposes a misleading conception of responsibility. It is the conception that I am concerned to set aside by suggesting that to declare that someone is responsible is to make a move in a practice. It is not to signal the presence in a person of some difficult-to-locate quality.

One indication that the line of questions is trending in the wrong direction is that the farther we move toward the purely private and undetectable, the willing and setting oneself to will, the farther we are from the sort of thing for which people are in fact held liability responsible. There are no rules against willing or setting oneself to will to pull a brake cord. There are rules that prohibit stopping a train when there is no scheduled stop or signal to stop. So somehow, by following this metaphysical lead, we are so far from pinning down the locus of responsibility that we are wandering outside of the realm in which questions of responsibility meaningfully arise. The metaphysical moves suggest that what is to be located, in determining "responsibility" of a person, is some fact about the person that by itself is a sufficient condition of the truth of the claim that she is responsible. Responsibility is, on that conception, a predicate like *round* or *blue*. But we have seen reason to believe otherwise: that to say of a person that she is responsible is to make a move within the context of a practice.

CONCLUSION

This chapter traced some of the moves that would be necessary in marshaling an adequate response to skepticism concerning legal or moral responsibility. It attempted to show that "responsible" is a practice-embedded term, a term not easily intelligible outside the confines of an understood practice. It is not a label like *sweet* or *brittle*, but more like *in check* or (in baseball) *out* or *safe*.

The point of showing this is to make clear that sweeping doubts about responsibility must be translated into doubts about the practice in which ascriptions of responsibility are possible. The question whether anyone "really is" responsible then becomes a query concerning the justifiability of this or that form of the practice. That is the question we will pursue. But first, in Chapter 6, we will cover the large topic of the sorts of defense that can be offered under the practice of Liability Responsibility.

That topic attended to, what then needs justification is not merely the practice according to which it is determined that people are liability-responsible but the compound practices that combine that finding with the imposition of a response: punishment, blame, or the requirement that a loss be made good. It is useful then to distinguish responsibility practices according to the response in question. I therefore continue to speak of Liability Responsibility as the morally neutral practice of determining where responsibility lies and of Punishment Responsibility, Compensation Responsibility, and Blame Responsibility as the compound practices consisting of the finding of liability plus the imposition of a particular sort of response.

CHAPTER 6

Defenses

Let us suppose that, as Mrs. O'Leary milks her cow Bessie in the dark of early morning, Bessie kicks Mrs. O'Leary's lantern into the hay and the resulting fire destroys the city of Chicago. Mrs. O'Leary can offer a number of different kinds of defense. She can claim immunity or incapacity, or she can offer an excuse or a justification. Some of these defenses may exonerate her; some may only mitigate the offense; and some may not be acceptable at all and have no effect. Let us look at these possibilities.

IMMUNITY

Mrs. O'Leary may contend that the finger should point somewhere else, or nowhere at all, because she is by virtue of her position not liable. She is the Consul General of Ireland and has diplomatic immunity. She is thus not subject to the criminal jurisdiction of Cook County, Illinois, nor of any other jurisdiction in the United States. She has a shield against ascriptions of liability, and she is exhibiting her shield. A king might have such a shield, contending that he is above the law. English traders claimed such immunity in nineteenth-century Shanghai. The "right of clergy" once provided limited immunity from criminal prosecution.

Claiming immunity is like claiming that one can't be put out at home plate because one is an umpire and not a player. The claimant is just not subject to the rules under which someone is attempting to hold him liable. The finger of imputation is pointing out of bounds, beyond the circle of those who need answer or suffer a response. Immunity is a defense that says the claimant need offer no further defense. It is a demand that one's status or standing be recognized and that the inquiry about one's liability stop there.

EXCUSE

Mrs. O'Leary may offer an excuse. She may say that the fire started by *accident*. To make good that excuse, she would be expected to show that she had taken the precautions against an accident that a "reasonable man" would have taken: she had placed the lantern on a shelf where no one could have predicted that (newly purchased, double-jointed) Bessie could reach it.

She can claim she started the fire under *compulsion*: Her brutal husband, harboring a grudge against all citizens of Chicago, forced her to place the lantern just where Bessie would kick it over on the hay. She can claim *mistake*: She had reasonably supposed that she was placing the lantern on an asbestos mat instead of in the hay.

She can contend that she was *ignorant* of some relevant fact. She was new at milking and did not know the grumpy nature of cows. She cannot plead ignorance of the law that requires only electric lighting in cowsheds. Ignorance of the law is in general not a legal excuse.

In offering an excuse, Mrs. O'Leary is conceding that what she has done is wrong. She has, by placing the lantern where she did, caused the Chicago Fire. But she offers a plea that will either exonerate her for the wrongdoing or will mitigate the response she would otherwise receive — thirty days in jail, say, rather than two years.

JUSTIFICATION

On the other hand, Mrs. O'Leary may argue that, despite appearances, what she did was not wrong but right. She can attempt to show that under the law she is required to have adequate lighting in her cowshed and that the only possible source, given no electrical supply, was a lantern. Or she can argue that common usage from time immemorial sanctions lanterns in cowsheds. Or that the record shows that it is safer to use lanterns than electric lights (whose connections in Chicago have often been faulty).

By similar reasoning, the captain of a ship can argue that he did right in jettisoning the cargo because if he had not done so the ship would have sunk; or the public health officer might attempt to justify restricting a person to her house because she is a leper.

INCAPACITY

Mrs. O'Leary may argue, or someone may argue for her, that she is ineligible to be held liable because she does not come up to some standard. She is not, or temporarily was not, a normal adult in full possession of her powers; she lacks, or lacked, the capacities a person should have if she is to be held liable. She was at the time (it having taken years to bring the case to trial) *Miss* O'Leary, aged ten. Or she was, and is, senile or feebleminded. She was suffering the aftereffects of an epileptic attack and did not know where she had placed the lantern. She had been heavily medicated and not fully aware of what she was doing. Or Bessie had first kicked her in the head, and she was unconscious when she placed the lantern in the hay.

By far the most controversial incapacity plea is that of insanity. Mrs. O'Leary can plead that at the time she was milking the cow she was insane and thus not responsible for whatever she may have done with her lantern.

THE DEFINITION OF INSANITY

It is obviously important to be able to distinguish bad persons from mad persons. If someone fires a pistol at the president or attacks the pope with a knife, he may be a hired killer, a treasonous conspirator, or a religious fanatic. But he may also be so mentally deranged that he believes he must do these things in self-defense, that the president or the pope, or perhaps both of them together, have cast a spell upon him that he can only exorcize by killing them. Neither retributivists nor utilitarians have good reason to favor punishing the insane: retributivists because they do not deserve it and utilitarians because it serves no deterrent purpose. On both views, if a person is certifiably insane and if his insanity accounts for his deed, then he is more properly sent to a mental institution than to prison. The retributivist emphasis on respect for persons seems to require it because he may need protection and treatment. The utilitarian concern for the general happiness implies that the dangerously insane be segregated and treated. From both points of view, it is therefore important that the mad be distinguished from the bad. But, as can easily be shown, that is not a simple matter.

THE M'NAGHTEN RULES

What are the criteria by which an appeal to insanity can be justified? A survey of some of the criteria that have been offered points up the difficulties in finding a satisfactory answer to this question. We begin with the best-known and most widely influential test of insanity, the *M'Naghten Rules*.

In 1843 in England, Daniel M'Naghten shot Edward Drummond, secretary to the prime minister, in the back. Drummond later died, and M'Naghten came to trial for murder. It appeared that M'Naghten believed that he was shooting the prime minister, whom he blamed for what he believed to be a Tory plot against his, M'Naghten's, life. There was political turmoil at the time, and it was widely believed that the shooting was a political assassination attempt against the prime minister. There was therefore an outcry when Lord Chief Justice Tindal stopped the trial, and the jury under his charge brought in a verdict of "not guilty on the ground of insanity." The House of Lords debated the question of what should be the grounds of a verdict of this kind and asked the judges to answer several questions about the insanity plea. In the response, Justice Tindal offered the following test of insanity:

> . . . . [I]t must be clearly proved that, at the time of committing the act, the accused was laboring under such a defect of reason, from disease of the mind, as not to know the nature and quality of the act he was doing, or, if he did know it, that he did not know he was doing what was wrong. (Morris, p. 395; *Rules*, p. 209)

These M'Naghten Rules prevailed for more than 100 years in English and American law and still have weight in the revision of federal and state law. The emphasis of the rules is on what M'Naghten *knew* when he shot Drummond or, rather, on what he did not know. What were the *facts* of which M'Naghten was ignorant? He thought that Drummond was the prime minister; and perhaps he believed that the "prime minister" was about to order troops to capture and kill him, M'Naghten. Or perhaps he believed that he had been anointed by God to save the world and that the prime minister, by seeking to kill him, was endangering the salvation of the world. Or perhaps he did not know that if he shot a person in the back that person would likely die. So much for knowledge of facts; but he might also qualify as insane if, knowing the relevant facts, he did not know that to shoot a person is *wrong*. He might have thought it no more wrong than swatting a fly. Finally, if he is to count as insane, his failures of knowledge of fact and of right and wrong must have resulted from "disease of the mind."

Given these suppositions about what M'Naghten thought he knew, it is hard to believe that any jury would fail to find him insane. So what is wrong with the M'Naghten Rules? Why should there be a search for a more satisfactory test? A serious difficulty is that the test is too narrow. It does not capture the full range of conditions that now count as mentally abnormal. This is because the whole emphasis of the test is on what the wrongdoer knew. It is a cognitive test, having to do with cognition, or knowing. But failures of knowledge are only a part of the story. The insane may also suffer from failure of the will, conative failures. A person may pass the M'Naghten test and still be insane because even if she knows what a normal person would know, she may be unable to resist doing what she knows is wrong. She may not be merely weak-willed, as most of us are in too many situations, but pathologically unable to control herself.

Suppose now that M'Naghten knew that he was killing someone, knew that it was Drummond, and knew that it was wrong to kill. Might he not still be insane? Perhaps so, if his problem was a conative one. Suppose that M'Naghten, when he shot Drummond, was on one of a series of manic highs of elation and overactivity that had characterized his adult life. Suppose that in this state he found himself with gun in hand, Drummond within range, and an overwhelming desire to fire the gun at Drummond—a desire so overwhelming that he was incapable of resisting it. Or suppose that, although he thinks it is wrong to kill and recognizes the danger, he is so depressed that he does not care whether someone may be killed by the random shots he fires out of his window.

ALTERNATIVE DEFINITIONS

The argument over the M'Naghten Rules sets the stage for a whole series of moves in the jurisprudence of insanity. One move is to supplement the M'Naghten Rules in such a way as to capture the class of persons whose will is in some way defective. The "irresistible impulse rule" states that "the accused must be capable not only of distinguishing between right and wrong, but that he was not impelled to do the act by an irresistible impulse. . . ." This rule, originated in the Court of Appeals in the District of Columbia in 1929, was found inadequate by the same court in 1954. The obvious problem of application lay in the difficulty of distinguishing between an impulse impossible for the accused to resist and an impulse that he simply did not resist. In addition, as the court later pointed out, "the term 'irresistible impulse' . . . carries the misleading implication that 'diseased mental condition[s]' produce only sudden, momentary, or spontaneous inclinations to commit unlawful acts." This implication was found to be simply untrue because there are mental diseases such as melancholia or paranoia that are characterized by unshakable long-term moods or mood shifts and may allow the painstaking planning of a crime over a period of time.

The inadequacy even of the irresistible impulse–supplemented M'Naghton Rule led, as might be expected, to an apparently less external test, a test that focuses more on the underlying causes of criminal behavior. This test, originated in New Hampshire in 1870 and adopted by the D. C. Court of Appeals in 1954, is that "an accused is not criminally responsible if his unlawful act was the product of mental disease or mental defect." This rule, named after the defendant in the case of *Durham v. United States* (Durham, 1954), is commonly known as the Durham Product Rule. The defects of this rule stem from the fact that the determination of insanity is left where it may seem to belong, to the experts, the psychiatrists. The first defect is that it is common for forensic psychiatrists (those who customarily testify in court) to be called for both the prosecution and the defense. Not only does this throw the supposedly scientific decision whether the act was the product of the disease back to the jury, but also suspicions arise about the scientific standing of psychiatric analysis because of the disagreements of psychiatrists over the difficult-to-decide cases that tend to wind up in court. A related defect is that psychiatric dispute is exacerbated by the requirement on psychiatric witnesses that they pronounce on the nature of the act in question as a "product." But *product* is not a term with any clear scientific meaning and is in fact a legal invention. This leads to a third defect: Supposing that the jury is not confused by conflicting psychiatric testimony, it may rely heavily on the "expert" testimony as to whether an act is the "product" of mental illness. But, because the decision whether the act is or is not a "product" is not strictly a scientific one, this is misplaced reliance.

At this point, the same court (by now the arbiter, however vacillating, of the test for insanity) decides in favor of what was already becoming a common standard: the American Law Institute's Model Penal Code definition. That code, under the heading "Mental Disease or Defect Excluding Responsibility" states the following:

1. A person is not responsible for criminal conduct if at the time of such conduct as a result of mental disease or defect he lacks substantial capacity either to appreciate the criminality [wrongfulness] of his conduct or to conform his conduct to the requirements of law.

2. As used in this Article, the terms "mental disease or defect" do not include an abnormality manifested only by repeated criminal or otherwise antisocial conduct. (*Model Penal Code*, Sec. 4.01)

This formulation of the insanity test wisely incorporates both cognitive and conative criteria. The wrongdoer must not only "know" but must "appreciate" that her deed is criminal (thus excluding the ambiguity of "wrong" between moral wrongdoing and illegal behavior). She must also have the power to resist what she "appreciates" as criminal behavior. It retains the requirement that her mental deficiency must be the result of mental disease but does not, like the Durham Product Rule, make that the sole criterion of insanity.

The drafters of the Model Penal Code reject the proposal of the majority of the Royal Commission on Capital Punishment, to

> leave to the jury to determine whether at the time of the act the accused was suffering from disease of the mind (or mental deficiency) to such a degree that he ought not to be held responsible. (Morris, p. 422; *Royal Commission on Capital Punishment, 1949–53*)

That proposal simply abandons the attempt to define insanity and leaves it up to the jury to decide, without guidance, whether the insanity plea should exonerate the wrongdoer, given the facts about the "disease of the mind" she suffers.

THE RATIONALE OF DEFENSES

As should be apparent from our discussion of Barbara Wootton's advocacy of a strict liability system of criminal law, the question can be raised why we need accept *any* defenses. Why not be satisfied to establish Mrs. O'Leary's contributory fault in the devastation of Chicago by fire? What is gained by taking into consideration her pleas for exoneration or mitigation on grounds of immunity, excuse, justification, or incapacity? In Chapter 4, we attributed Wootton's interest in eliminating defenses to her belief that the criminal law should be made more manageable, a better instrument for the control of behavior. Defenses have, on her view, to do with the establishment of fault, but concern with fault is an anachronism that should have no role in the criminal law. The law is not for the purpose of finding fault or assessing blame but to advance the social good by encouraging good behavior instead of bad. This is close to the view of B. F. Skinner, for whom the supreme issue is the efficiency of social control.

There is another point of view from which any advocacy of defenses is suspect. Friedrich Nietzsche argues for a "community of the strong." The strong are unconcerned with pardon and forgiveness, with nattering discussions about who is at fault. The strong are governed by self-imposed draconic laws, laws reminiscent of Hammurabi's Code, in which the sole question is whether the code has been violated. True, questions of immunity and justification will arise because these defenses are bastions of the community of the strong. But excuses and pleas of incapacity are for the weak and should have no weight in such a community (Nietzsche, Sec. 257 ff.).

At least three different sorts of arguments have been given why the criminal law *should* leave room for defenses. The first, offered by Jerome Hall, is that there should be no liability to punishment unless what the person has done is morally wrong. That is, moral wrongdoing is a necessary but not a sufficient condition of justified punishment (Hall, Ch. V). But in the absence of defenses, we have no idea whether Mrs. O'Leary has done what is morally wrong. Hence, defenses should be allowed. The difficulty here is in demonstrating Hall's first premise. A good deal more argument is necessary to establish its truth. To say nothing more, there are, as we have seen, utilitarian arguments for a social policy of strict liability for certain offenses that are very damaging to the common welfare. If these arguments are well founded and if social well-being is a properly moral end of policy, there may be good moral reasons for at least limited, strict liability legislation.

Hall's argument (and that of Lord Justice Denning) turns on the meaning of the legal term *mens rea*. That term is something of a weasel word in jurisprudential debate. A well-known but ambiguous legal maxim is that *actus non est reus nisi mens sit rea*. Literally, "the act is not bad unless the mind is bad." Lord Denning interprets that maxim as implying that "in order than an act should be punishable, it must be morally blameworthy, it must be a sin." But the maxim may also be read as implying, if not simply stating, that no one should be punished unless he intends to do the act, as intention is interpreted in penal statute or common law. *Mens rea* when understood in that way becomes a legally bad or guilty mind, rather than a morally bad one (Hart, 1968, p. 36).

Jeremy Bentham argues that in a well-constructed legal system there will be an "economy of threats." The overall purpose of the criminal law, as of any utilitarian social policy, is to maximize happiness and minimize misery. To introduce empty or useless threats into a legal system is to weaken the force of the meaningful threats that are necessary if the system is to be effective. There will be less apprehension of the threatened punishments. But threats directed to infants or the insane are empty. They are not capable of being influenced by them. Thus, infancy and insanity are allowable defenses. So also it is an allowable defense to plead, in justification, that had one not disobeyed a law there would have been an "instant calamity." On the same line of argument, Bentham finds utilitarian reasons to support the defenses of unintentionality, unconsciousness, mistake, ignorance, and compulsion (Bentham, Ch. 13).

H. L. A. Hart holds that the value of defenses (he is particularly concerned with excuses) lies in their protection of the freedom of the individual under law. Each person must be given as much room as possible to determine her own course of life. A civilized criminal justice system will not try merely to compel behavior but will rather attempt to give people "reasons for exercising choice in the direction of obedience, but leaving them to choose." A legal system that includes defenses is a better system for maximizing individual choice—what to do and how to live—rather than one that eliminates defenses. This is so mainly because life under a strict liability system is far less predictable than under one that allows defenses for lawbreaking.

> But if we are . . . to be liable if we strike someone by accident, by mistake, under coercion, etc., the chances that we shall incur the sanctions are immeasurably increased. From our knowledge of the past career of our body considered as a *thing*, we cannot infer much as to the chances of its being brought into violent contact with another, and under a system that dispensed with the excusing conditions of, say, accident (implying lack of intention) a collision alone would land us in jail. (Hart, 1968, p. 48)

This rationale of defenses is independent of and can even come in conflict with that offered by Bentham. We have already noted that there can be and is disagreement between utilitarians about the utility of defenses. If the abolishment of defenses were shown to maximize happiness, Bentham would be committed to abolishment. Choices are not to be maximized, on Hart's view, as a way of increasing happiness but because it is a fundamental principle that each person should have as much freedom as possible, consistent with the freedom of others, to plan his own life. So even at the cost of overall happiness, there would be reason for retaining defenses.

CONCLUSION

In this chapter, we considered the variety of defenses that can be marshaled within the practice of responsibility–ascription. This is necessary as a way of fleshing out the practice and of opening up the philosophical topic of responsibility beyond the bounds of freedom versus determinism. The practice, curtailed or elaborated, is very old and very widespread. What it would mean to declare someone responsible independently of the practice is far from clear. Among the defenses, we gave special attention to a particularly controversial one, the plea of insanity, and traced the development of that plea in this and the last century. Finally, we examined the various arguments that have been offered as to why we should have defenses at all, why we should not settle for a strict liability system of criminal law.

We now turn to the question of how, if at all, the practice we have placed under our philosophical magnifying glass can be justified. It will not do for a philosopher just to say that it is long-lived and widespread. What are the reasons, if any, why it should not be abolished or radically altered?

Does Responsibility Have a Future?

How, if at all, can the practice of ascribing personal responsibility for harm be justified? What sort of argument, if any, might convince skeptics that it deserves to survive? One suggestion to be explored here is that justification might start from the question of how losses are to be distributed.

THE CHALLENGE

As we have seen, the force of much of the metaphysical and "scientific" attack on Liability Responsibility lies in the question of whether any person is responsible for what he does. If no one is responsible, then the practice of holding people liable to response is, so the argument goes, morally destitute. People are not responsible because they can't help doing what they do; and we can't justifiably hold people liable for what they can't help doing. Until it is established that people *can* help what they do, the skeptical argument assumes, the most that can be shown is that it is sometimes useful to hold persons responsible, even though there is no moral justification for doing so. But because no conclusive argument has been found that people can help doing what they do and are hence morally responsible, the future of moral and legal responsibility is and ought to be very much in question.

In approaching the question of whether personal responsibility can be justified and thus whether it deserves to have a future or to shrivel away as an outmoded vestige of the past, we must ask what kind of answer, if any, would be satisfactory to the skeptic. This requires distinguishing, among the skeptics, between the hard determinists, who say that no one can ever help doing what she is doing, and those nonmetaphysical determinists, who hold only that some large percentage of people cannot help what they do.

It is clear that nothing short of a demonstration of the falsity of a hoary metaphysical doctrine would satisfy the hard determinists. If hard determinism were true, there would appear to be a "metaphysical stop" on any further moral inquiry about responsibility. We could not take up the justification of personal responsibility without first resolving the metaphysical question. But because there are other determinists who concede that at least some people can help doing what they do some of the time, there is for them no immovable metaphysical boulder in the way of discussing the moral merits of personal responsibility–ascription. We therefore address those skeptics who are not hard determinists. Most scientific determinists fall into this class. They are more likely to speak of the degree of probability that particular persons will engage in wrongdoing than of the inevitability that they will.

The challenge then is to show these nonhard determinists (and skeptics who may not be determinists at all, like the practical, moral, and technological skeptics mentioned in Chapter 4) that there is a moral argument worth taking seriously why personal responsibility should not be allowed to shrivel away. What kind of argument? It amounts to a comparison of practices on moral grounds—an argument that, among the available alternatives, personal responsibility deserves consideration. It is not a proof. It does not dispose of the metaphysical stop. It does not claim comprehensiveness in its survey of alternative practices or combinations of practices because I do not know any way of showing that all possible alternative practices have been considered. The argument can at most show that, among the main types of practice, the ascription of personal responsibility is a morally defensible alternative. It does not establish the sole claim to moral approbation among the possible practices with which it is contrasted. The argument leaves open the option that personal responsibility may be supplemented by or may supplement alternative practices. Finally, it confines its claims to a certain class of situations, as we will see. Nevertheless, within these limits, the case that can be made for the practice of personal responsibility–ascription is a compelling one.

PRELIMINARIES

Our focus here is not on liability to imprisonment or fines but on liability to make restitution or to offer compensation. We therefore take as our beginning place situations more characteristic of torts than of criminal law, in which there has been a loss attributable in some degree to wrongdoing, where the question is not so much what the wrongdoer deserves to suffer as what he must make good. The advantage of this approach is that there may be better reasons to doubt the moral justifiability of punishment responses than of responses requiring restitution or compensation. Although I argued in Part One that punishment can be justified, there is no reason why the case for personal responsibility should rest on that claim. To many informed and reflective people, the infliction of punishment will still seem morally questionable. But there is a readily visible moral point in compensation. This is not to concede that punishment is morally unjustifiable but to recognize that there are deep-going differences on that subject, differences that tend to distort discussion of personal responsibility, because the latter practice may be justifiable whatever one's opinion may be of punishment. The two overall justifying aims of personal responsibility–ascription, punitive and compensatory, are, however, closely related.

Although it is safe to characterize Anglo-American criminal law today as primarily punitive in intent, the long history of that law reveals a pendulum swing from compensatory responses to wrongdoing toward punitive responses and now an apparent swing back toward compensatory ones. This fact is of some importance for the sort of justification I suggest for personal responsibility–ascription as a practice. The scope of that justification may extend further over what today is typically considered criminal law than is at first apparent.

In speaking of losses, we speak of harms under a certain aspect, or from a certain point of view. In asking what has been lost in suffering a harm, we are typically trying to assess the harm for the purpose of doing something about it. Not every harm can be made good by restitution, but compensation can be offered for any harm — even though we may consider some harms impossible to fully (or even minimally) compensate. Thus, every harm can be considered a loss; but it is more natural to speak of losses where there is some point in speaking of making good the harm done through compensation. On this understanding, we can speak meaningfully of losses even though there is no reasonable hope that the particular person who brought about the loss (through her contributory fault) can make it good. It may have to be made good in some other way than by compensation from the wrongdoer. Mrs. O'Leary, we can assume, is not going to be able to make good the loss of Chicago.

This brings us to a survey of the ways in which this "making good" through compensation might be done. The purpose of the survey is, as I have suggested, to show that personal responsibility is a practice not easily eliminated when the moral merits of the alternatives are examined.

We now specify a little more closely the practice of personal responsibility for loss (Compensation Responsibility, for short) as it is to be defended here. Assuming that a loss has been suffered by someone and that B has "brought about" that loss (it having come about through his contributory fault), B must make good the loss that person has suffered. The response to his wrongdoing is the requirement that he make good the loss. If he cannot make it good through restitution, he must do so through compensation. It may be either that, like Mrs. O'Leary, B is unable to compensate for the loss or that the loss is simply beyond compensation, like the loss of a friendship or a marriage. To say that B is liable to make good the loss is to say that, given that the loss can be made good and that it is within B's power at least partially to make it good, B must do what he can to compensate the victim. That requirement is the response to which B is liable.

LAISSEZ-TOMBER

The general problem with which we are concerned is how losses should be distributed. It is interesting and central to the present argument that there is no way of avoiding the choice of a practice or practices for the allocation of losses. Suppose someone says, "We won't have a practice, we'll just let losses lie where they fall." Then we must reply that letting losses lie where they fall is itself a practice. According to that practice, when a person suffers a loss, no matter how the loss happened, no matter whether someone else's fault contributed to the loss, there will be no question of anyone else's sharing the loss or attempting to make it good. Instead, the loss will be borne entirely by the person whose loss it is. It would be easy to explain the practice, which we will call *laissez-tomber*, to interested Martians.

Because the choice of a practice for the allocation of losses is unavoidable and the skeptic objects to Compensation Responsibility as a practice, then she may fairly be asked which practice she regards as morally preferable to Compensation Responsibility. Of course, elimination of alternatives on moral grounds will not close off the debate because there is no argument to show that all possible practices have been considered. But the argument can have a kind of practical conclusiveness. Given that there is a problem of choice and that the skeptic objects on moral grounds to Compensation Responsibility as a way of dealing with it, she must give reasons for morally preferring some other practice(s). The burden of proof is then on her to come up with candidates for a morally acceptable practice. What is that practice going to be?

Before turning to the various answers that could be given to that question, we must say what, for present purposes, we count as reasons for holding one practice to be morally less desirable than another. I suggest two such types of reason. The first is that it, more than the practices with which it is being compared, tends to encourage indifference to the interests of other persons. The second (and closely related) reason is that, under the practice in question, to a greater degree than under the practice with which it is being compared, the wrongdoer is allowed or encouraged to make a special case of himself in that he may violate generally obeyed and widely beneficial rules when it suits his own interest to do so. For short, I refer to the first of these criteria of moral preferability as the Indifference Criterion and to the second as the Special-Case Criterion. The Indifference Criterion is closely related to the Categorical Imperative of Immanuel Kant, who maintains, in the second formulation of that imperative, that one should never treat persons as mere means to one's objectives, but always as "ends in themselves" (Kant, Section II). The Special-Case Criterion is implied by the general, and widely accepted, rule of justice that relevantly like cases should be treated alike and relevantly different cases should be treated differently.

The practices we will examine here, with an eye to their comparative moral acceptability, are possible or actual general practices. They are general not only in the sense that they admit of many forms, but also in the senses that, once adopted and incorporated into the law, they are likely to persist for a considerable period of time, and that, because they are a part of the law that covers a great many cases, they affect a large number of people.

It is a part of our hypothetical choice between practices that we are talking about losses where there is contributory fault of a person. We are not concerned with losses that result from natural disasters, say, or "acts of God." Our concern here is with losses that are brought about by a person or persons, where there is no question about the presence or absence of an adequate defense to exempt, exonerate, or mitigate. We stipulate, for purposes of our inquiry, that there is no viable defense. Let us return, then, to *laissez-tomber*.

Morgan, let us say, brings about a loss to Astor. He brings the loss about by allowing his herbicide to drift over her farm, by forcing her into a ditch by his chancy passing on a highway, by installing a very loud loudspeaker across the road from her previously quiet home, or by sending Astor to the hospital with lung cancer caused by emissions from his air-polluting plant. With respect to such cases, which are generalizable to the very large class of cases in which interests conflict, *laissez-tomber* fails the indifference test in that, because losses *will* lie where they fall, no motive is provided under the practice to look out for the interests of others. Morgan may happily go about his business ignoring the possibility or probability that he may cause losses to Astor or to anyone else.

The application of the Special-Case Criterion is less direct. Because, under *laissez-tomber*, the rule is that Morgan may pursue his interests without regard to the losses of others, Morgan is not making a special case of himself in following that rule. But would Morgan want such a rule, a rule that would permit Astor and everyone else to ignore his, Morgan's, interests where loss to him is possible or probable? We may well doubt that, and in doubting suspect that what Morgan really wants is that while other people should look out for his interests, he should not have to look out for theirs.

Nevertheless, we cannot entirely discount the value, even the moral defensibility, of *laissez-tomber* where the loss is trivial. There, the secondary costs (the dislocations that redistribution of losses may cause) could well be minimized by taking no action to redistribute the loss. This consideration may qualify our judgment as defenders of Compensation Responsibility that the wrongdoer should be required to make restitution to or to compensate the victim. To extend Compensation Responsibility to trivial cases might be to exhibit indifference to the overall interests of the persons falling under the practice. If we were regularly to hold people liable for splashing mud on others' shoes, for misspelling names, or for dialling telephone numbers by mistake, the expense and inconvenience to everyone of such a system of claims might well not be worth the trivial gains of a few.

ARBITRARY ALLOCATION AND GROUP LIABILITY

In reflecting on the general problem of a morally justifiable allocation of losses, it becomes apparent that there are only a few general types of practice to consider.

We can adopt *laissez-tomber*, or we can assign liability for compensation to a person, a group, or the community as a whole. The assignment of that liability may be arbitrary or nonarbitrary. I will not attempt to scout all of the possible subheadings under these general classifications or their possible combinations. Here I offer some remarks on arbitrary allocation of losses and about allocation to groups; then I turn to allocation to the community as a whole. My overall purpose is to make clear to the skeptic about Compensation Responsibility that, if he thinks there are moral defects in the ascription of personal liability for loss, he should recognize that there are moral difficulties inherent in the other main types of loss allocation too. His argument cannot be solely a negative one, a moral critique of Compensation Responsibility, but it must also be one that faces the positive problem of what practice or combination of practices is morally preferable to personal liability for loss. Losses must be allocated somehow. How are they to be distributed?

Under arbitrary allocation of losses, Bass may be designated as the person to make good the losses brought about by Morgan and suffered by Astor. The arbitrary assignment to Bass of the duty to make Astor's losses good may be by fiat or by a fair procedure like a well-conducted lottery. If by fiat, some fourth person, Dexter, would have the power to decide who is to make good any loss. I think it need not be argued that allocation by fiat would be morally indefensible. On the other hand, we can imagine arbitrary allocation with safeguards against the ugly possibilities inherent in allocation by fiat. For example, we can imagine a public lottery in which, by carefully supervised methods, the loss suffered by a person is allocated to some person or persons who need have nothing whatever to do with the bringing about of the loss. Bass is simply the loser upon whom the loss descends. He will have to have Astor's car repaired or pay for her hospital bills.

It is reasonably obvious that this practice, too, fails the moral tests. Morgan would have no more motive than under *laissez-tomber* to look out for Astor's interests as he pursues his own. He would, by the same line of reasoning, be making a special case of himself. That is (unless he is willing to gamble with his own possible ruin through the unpredictable descent upon himself of someone else's losses), he would be happy for others to subscribe to this practice, but he would not be happy to be obliged to abide by it himself.

The moral faultiness of this practice is akin to the immorality of slavery. No matter what she may do to avoid loss to others, a person could be legally bound to another, bound to exert her efforts for the benefit of the other, until the loss has been made good. A central aim of allocating losses is to avoid, or mitigate the effects of, situations in which losses brought about by others may disastrously affect the person suffering the loss. But arbitrary allocation, however fairly administered, does nothing to accomplish that end. By shifting the task of making good the loss to some arbitrarily chosen person or persons, there is no gain over *laissez-tomber*. Nothing the individual could do would reduce the chance that she would nevertheless have to make good someone else's loss, and thereby herself be a loser. In a public loss lottery, then, we would have an example of a morally indefensible practice that still could be fairly administered. Its fair administration would allow it to avoid the criticisms of arbitrary allocation by fiat, but it would not for all that be morally acceptable.

With respect to group compensatory liability, it may be sufficient to note that allocation to arbitrarily chosen groups shares the moral defects of all arbitrary allocation. Some nonarbitrary allocations of losses to groups are, by our criteria, quite acceptable, however. Insurance schemes voluntarily entered and fairly administered may violate neither of our criteria. They need not encourage indifference to the interests of others nor the making of a special case of oneself.

That group compensatory liability cannot serve as a universal substitute for personal compensatory liability, however, is evident for two reasons. The first is that there are circumstances appropriate for personal responsibility for loss that are not appropriate for group liability. Whereas group liability may be useful, say, to hedge insurable risks, it is less useful or not useful at all as protection against harassment of one individual by another, or against trespass, or against obscene acts. Secondly, even in those circumstances in which group compensatory liability obtains, personal responsibility may well be the practice within the group. Even if the group may have to answer for and bear the losses brought about by some member, the member may well be required to answer to the group and be expected to bear a heavy share of the group's burden in making good the loss. For example, if he habitually causes losses, under a common insurance scheme, his premiums are likely to rise accordingly.

UNIVERSAL NO-FAULT INSURANCE SCHEME

A conceivable, and philosophically interesting, mode of allocating losses is to spread them across a whole community, even a national community. Let us define a Universal No-Fault Insurance Scheme as a practice in which, when someone suffers a loss, there is no inquiry concerning contributory fault. Rather, the question is whether and to what degree the loss can be made good, it being understood that the loss-sufferer will be compensated out of a fund to which he or she and all of the other members of the community contribute. For simplicity, we speak only of monetary compensation, and leave open the formula by which it is calculated how much each member contributes to the fund.

As we contemplate the adoption of some such scheme, we realize that it could not be adopted without at least one important qualification, a qualification that has many ramifications. It is that we exclude losses that the sufferer brings upon himself. Suppose that we included losses that are the result of the sufferer's own negligence, rashness, foolishness, imprudence, or simple lack of concern to avoid losses. Suppose that the loss-causer (and sufferer) is simply indifferent about the conduct of his own affairs to the point that he does not worry about losses since he knows that he will be compensated? Suppose that he is inordinately greedy and enters into all sorts of marginal business ventures, unguarded contracts, and one-sided trades? A system that encouraged this sort of behavior by compensating self-inflicted losses would surely court ruin. The burden of losses would be greater than it could bear. But allowing self-inflicted losses to qualify for compensation would also be morally questionable. It would encourage a cavalier attitude toward the interests of others, because the sure-to-be-compensated self-inflictor of loss would, by his carelessness, recklessness, or greed also be likely to burden others with losses.

It follows that at least some inquiry must be made concerning contributory fault, even in this most extreme version of loss-spreading. The class of losses suffered at least partially through one's own fault is, however, a large one, and the margin between self- and other-inflicted losses may, in given cases, be none too clear. For example, it is often hard to say to what extent my attitude toward others can bring about their inflicting losses upon me. It is even harder to say to what extent I bring about in myself the attitudes I have toward others.

In Universal No-Fault Insurance against loss then, the loss must have been brought about by some person or persons not identical with the loss-sufferer. The loss must be made good from a fund to which each member of the community contributes. But the person who brings about the loss has no more obligation than any other member of the community to make good the loss. She does her full share by contributing to the fund.

We should note that there are many situations in which wide loss-spreading will be morally defensible. It will be defensible in just those suituations in which questions of agency fade into the background. As we survey the smoldering ruins, it would be mere perverse curiosity or vengefulness that would lead us to spend time on the inquiry whether it was Mrs. O'Leary's or Mrs. Tooley's cow that kicked over the lantern in dry and wooden Chicago. There could be no meaningful question of compensation by either of those women. And while we might, and perhaps should, require compensation by a mugger, at the same time we would have to realize that this requirement is unlikely, because of the usual economic condition of muggers, to be much help to the victim. In either case, there seems to be a societal duty to take over where individual compensation fails or is likely to fail to meet the needs of the victim.

It is of some importance, though, to bring out as well as we can the moral contrast between Universal No-Fault Insurance and Compensation Responsibility because it is often the expansion of no-fault practices that, in current life, results in the contraction of the sphere of personal responsibility. This expansion is justified in some contexts, as I suggested in the previous paragraph. In general, it seems justified to require that everyone chip in to compensate losses that are unlikely to be compensable in any other way (supposing, as we have stipulated, that the loss is not self-caused). There are losses that, while brought about by other persons and while not "acts of God," nevertheless approximate natural disasters. As we have seen, the Chicago Fire would be an example; wartime bombing damage is another; and the environmental damage resulting from the widespread release of pollutants into the atmosphere is a third. Yet because such losses are not natural disasters and a human cause (even if a very diffuse or distant one) can be located, personal (or, more typically, group) responsibility does enter into the calculation of who should contribute what to the fund from which losses are compensated. Thus, the insurance rates of a tinder-dry, wooden Chicago will be higher than those of a Chicago built of masonry; wartime compensation is sought from the losers; and polluting plants are required, even at great expense, to purify their emissions.

It is arguable that such differential contributions to the insurance scheme are morally justified to the extent they fall on the human cause of the loss; and the argument that comes most readily to mind is that those who are responsible should pay most. But before turning to the moral credentials of Compensation Responsibility, let us tarry a bit with Universal No-Fault Insurance as a mode of loss-distribution.

It might be thought that the unfairness of the practice could be avoided by relying on the criminal law to deter careless surgeons, bullies, and profiteers—that a properly constructed set of criminal sanctions would limit the loss-claims against the common fund. That is, it might be felt that by prohibiting certain sorts of action or failures to act, under pain of criminal sanction, the field would be left clear for fair operation of Universal No-Fault Insurance. There are, however, two objections to that proposal.

The first is that the proposed practice would not so much then offer an alternative to personal liability for loss as a mode of shifting personal liability—from liability to make compensation to liability to suffer punishment. Because the justification of legal punishment is more debatable than the justification of the requirement that those who bring about losses should make them good, little or nothing is gained by the shift.

The second objection is that selfish, greedy, cruel, and careless actions would now have to be prosecutable offenses. Whereas, before, a person who through greediness had brought about a loss had a duty to offer compensation, now he must suffer punishment. But it remains to be shown that there is moral advance in moving from a practice that requires compensation to a practice that requires punishment, where the requirement of compensation might serve the same preventive end.

ANSWERABILITY AND THE MORAL COMMUNITY

A less obvious moral reason for rejecting Universal No-Fault Insurance is that it would, if accepted, undermine the existence of moral communities. It has been convincingly argued that moral communities are best understood as groups whose members are mutually answerable to one another for violating mutually agreed-on moral rules (Blatz, passim). In fact, we could understand moral rules as just those rules people may blame one another for violating, provided no adequate defense is offered. Demanding, giving, and assessing defenses would then not be accidental but necessary features of a moral community. There is a good deal to commend this conception of a moral community. It can provide an explanation of the way in which, however vaguely, we determine membership. Only persons may be members who recognize the need to answer for their conduct, that given modes of behavior constitute violations, and that the rules in question are rules. Non-members cannot be held accountable for the violation of rules because a necessary condition of accountability is the recognition that there are rules to violate.

This limitation on moral communities presupposes that it is possible to distinguish between people whose nonrecognition of a set of rules is attributable to lack of maturity or to unfortunate educational practices and people who do not recognize some rules in that they could give reasons for rejecting them even if the rules and their rationale were clear to them. The distinction, once made, does not preclude holding that there are moral considerations to which all people should pay heed in discussing the acceptability of rules and practices. Nor does it preclude holding that there are restrictions anyone should recognize as applying to herself and everyone else, restrictions for the violation of which she may rightly be held answerable.

By definition, Universal No-Fault Insurance bypasses the practice (or subpractice) of Compensation Liability because under the former practice there is no inquiry regarding fault. The vocabulary of the various forms of defense is eliminated. But, if the moral community is understood to be the community within which this language and vocabulary are employed, then to bypass answerability is to eliminate the moral community.

LIMITED NO-FAULT INSURANCE: THE COST OF ACCIDENTS

It might be objected to the argument against Universal No-Fault Insurance as a substitute for personal liability that it cuts too widely in that it would rule out closely related practices that seem to be not only desirable on consequential grounds but also morally acceptable. It might be asked why, if we are to reject that practice, we should not also have to reject no-fault insurance for automobile accidents. This objection requires that we glance at the latter practice and attempt to show why an argument from its acceptability to the acceptability of Universal No-Fault Insurance fails.

For present purposes, we define automobile no-fault insurance as a practice that accords to a person who suffers loss in a collision the right to recover his losses from his own insurance company without going to court to establish who was at fault for the accident. The defensibility of this practice hinges on its insuring us in an effective way against a nearly unavoidable hazard, a hazard against which personal liability provides only spotty and unreliable protection—distributing collision losses in an arguably evenhanded manner. Automobile no-fault insurance brings to the fore a third kind of case in which, although someone may be guilty of contributory fault, personal liability seems, taken alone, to provide little assurance that losses will be covered. The first two such cases were what we may call the O'Leary Case and the Mugger Case. In the first of these, the wrongdoer triggers, as anyone might, a common hazard (tinder-dry, wooden Chicago) and brings about a loss to many people. In the second, the type of wrongdoer who causes loss to individuals is unlikely to be able to make the loss good. In no-fault automobile insurance, by contrast, the person involved in a collision may or may not be at fault, but conditions are such that it is hard for anyone to avoid occasional fault.

Fault recedes into the background as it becomes more and more difficult to avoid collision, just as it recedes as large social forces provide impetus for the actions of individuals or as enormous consequences can explode from the small spark supplied by an individual's momentary carelessness. Even so, fault and personal liability do not disappear; and a practice like automobile no-fault insurance is accepted largely because personal liability cannot by itself be trusted to make good the nearly inevitable losses.

The ongoing discussion of losses from automobile collision is a rich source of ideas for the allocation of losses in general. It opens up a wide panorama of possible practices for the allocation of losses. Basically two methods are recognized: allocation by spreading the loss and allocation to the "deepest pockets." The former method requires "the accomplishment of the broadest possible spreading of losses over people and over time." The latter places losses "on those classes of people or activities that are best able to pay, usually the 'wealthiest,' regardless of whether this involves spreading" (Calabresi, p. 21). It is noteworthy that *apparently* neither of these methods places any special burden on the person who has brought about the loss. However, the special burden does not disappear. For one thing, if the loss is spread over drivers, it is commonly done so by means of an insurance scheme that allows the rates of drivers who have frequent collisions to soar.

All schemes for the allocation of losses from accidents must be judged as acceptable relative to the context in which they are to operate. If driving is necessary for livelihood and therefore nearly universally engaged in and accidents very difficult to avoid, then collision losses may be regarded in something of the same way as we regard losses from general conflagration or flood—as losses stemming from an unavoidable hazard of life and therefore as generally distributable in a community that has some concern for the general interest. (In my hometown, driving to work can be risky enough that bumper stickers read "Pray for me; I drive Highway 183.") But if, given an excellent public-transportation system, driving were unnecessary, if it were a luxury, like sailing or hang gliding, the context would be significantly different. Then the losses suffered might seem best borne by those who engage in the activity of driving. The interest O'Connor has in avoiding a loss from sailing is not an interest that anyone else has an obligation to honor, so O'Connor and fellow sailors must make appropriate arrangements to meet possible losses—by insuring against them. Then the cost of his insurance will be determined by the loss-record of sailboat owners in general and his in particular.

BACK TO DETERMINISM

The hard determinist denies that anyone may, within the bounds of morality, be held liable — that if the wrongdoer can't help doing what he does, he is not to blame, is not at fault, incurs no moral obligations as a consequence of what he has done. In particular, he incurs no obligation to make good losses to which his wrongdoing has been contributory, and although there may be utilitarian value in requiring him to make the loss good, there is no moral justification for requiring him to do so.

The counterargument of this chapter moves from the need for a practice to the relative moral acceptability of a practice. But if there must be a practice (for the allocation of losses) and if, of the available practices, personal liability is at least as morally acceptable as the alternatives, given the context, then its continuance as a practice is justified. Or if Compensation Responsibility in conjunction with other practices for the allocation of losses is an acceptable alternative, then it is justified. At any rate, the argument leaves the burden of proof on the skeptic to show that *her* way of allocating losses is fairer than allocating them by Compensation Responsibility.

Suppose now that we are hard determinists and that we compare *laissez-tomber* with Universal No-Fault Insurance. For us, no one is at fault, yet there are still losses to distribute. They can be spread or not. If they are not spread then, unless they are allocated to deep pockets, some people will suffer heavy losses that will be disastrous for them, and other people will suffer no losses at all. Does this not violate the principle that relevantly like cases be treated alike and different cases differently (a form of the Special-Case Criterion)? The injustice of *laissez-tomber* consists for us, as hard determinists, in the unevenness of the distribution of losses. The uneven distribution is unjust because some people (not through their fault because for us there is no fault) are quite arbitrarily set back in competition for nearly everything for which people compete: status, professional achievement, affection, goods, and services. This is then an unfair competition, one in which arbitrary distinctions between persons are allowed too much scope. But there is also suffering and frustration, the loss that is such not merely relative to the advantages of others but in itself. No one wants to suffer or be frustrated. If it is in our power to choose practices that allocate losses, it would be unjust to choose a practice that arbitrarily makes some people suffer greatly, in preference to a practice that spreads losses so widely that no one suffers much more than anyone else. This unfairness obtains quite independently of any moral responsibility for bringing about losses. Even if there is no moral responsibility for losses, there is competition and a general desire to avoid suffering and frustration. There is therefore still moral reason for us as hard determinists to prefer some practices to others.

For us as hard determinists, personal liability would, on the above line of reasoning, be unjust for essentially the same reason that *laissez-tomber* is unjust. It results in a lumpy rather than in an even distribution of losses. But a lumpy distribution results in the hardships mentioned. Personal liability is thus, for us, morally inferior to any practice that spreads losses so that no one suffers or so that everyone endures minimal suffering so that no one suffers severely.

In our discussion of hard determinism, I have granted for the sake of argument that it makes sense for a hard determinist to speak of choosing a practice. However, there is reason to believe that a consistent hard determinist cannot speak literally of choosing. For him we cannot help "choosing" as we do. But the notion of a choice we cannot help making in the way we do make it is difficult to understand.

Yet the hard determinist speaks of the elimination of personal liability. She apparently believes then that there is some morally preferable mode of allocating losses. If so, she believes that it is possible to choose one practice in preference to another. The critic with whom the defender of personal responsibility must deal appears then to be an inconsistent hard determinist: one who believes it possible to choose practices, but not to choose courses of action.

CONCLUSION

The outcome of the discussion of this part is that a person is liability-responsible if and only if he occupies a certain practice-defined position. The position is that of a person who has brought about harm and who lacks an acceptable defense for having done so. Given Liability Responsibility, it is yet to be determined what the response to liability will be. It is the compound practices, composed of Liability Responsibility plus a response (punishment, required compensation, or blame), that need moral justification. Liability Responsibility alone is incomplete, lacks a reference to a response, and thus is morally neutral. We elected to examine Compensation Responsibility, the compound practice of requiring persons who are liability-responsible for having brought about a loss to make compensation. The point that I have tried to make is that the decision whether to have such a practice is not arbitrary, that there are good reasons why it should be retained rather than abandoned or allowed to wither away.

The responses on which we have focused have been legal ones: punishment or required compensation. But there are nonlegal responses to Liability Responsibility — such as blame, disappointment, or outrage — that must have a place in any rounded account of personal responsibility. Responsibility–ascription is not only a matter of law but also of morality. In Part Three, we will consider the question of how, if at all, legal and moral concerns can be distinguished.

Law and Morality

CHAPTER 8

Law

We sometimes contrast what is legally with what is morally required. For example, it is morally but not legally required that we should be grateful to persons who have done us favors at considerable cost to themselves; and it is legally but not morally required that we register for the draft in an unjust war. There are tensions between morality and law. Some people would use the law to "enforce morality." Others would reject particular laws on moral grounds. Some insist that a "true," "real," or "valid" law must be morally justifiable. Others hold that the question of whether a purported rule of law is valid can only be answered by appeal to purely legal, nonmoral, criteria. In this and the succeeding chapters, we examine some of these tensions. Let us begin with the question, "What is law?" If we can say what law is, then perhaps we can say what does and does not fall within its boundaries and whether, and if so how, morality is to be found there.

LEGAL POSITIVISM AND LEGAL REALISM

An answer that may seem simple and above reproach is this one: Law is the set of rules that those in power lay down and enforce. But how in power and how enforced? Do we mean to include or exclude the rules that a supernatural being or beings may lay down for people? Let us say that we mean to discuss only the rules that people set for people. Then how do we mean that the rules are enforced? By public opinion, say, or by the threat of fines and imprisonment? Let's take the latter option because what we want to talk about are the rules that *governments* lay down and enforce, and governments can't rely on public opinion about lawbreaking as their means of enforcement. At any rate, even if they try to marshal public opinion behind the law, they must have at their disposal a credible threat of force. So our amended definition is that law is the set of rules that governments lay down and enforce by the threat of penalties, including prison and fines.

This is still a very inadequate definition of law. It comes closest to adequacy as a definition of criminal law. However, it epitomizes the view of a most influential movement in British and American legal history: the legal positivist movement. John Austin (1790–1859) is the best-known ancestor of that movement. In *The Province of Jurisprudence Determined*, Austin marks off what he calls "positive law" from every other sort of law with which it might be confused:

> [T]he essential difference of a positive law . . . may be stated thus. Every positive law, or every law simply and strictly so called, is set by a sovereign person, or a sovereign body of persons, to a member or members of the independent political society wherein that person or body is sovereign or supreme. (Lecture VI)

To be sovereign or supreme is to be able to enforce one's desires about how others should behave. Sovereigns are just those persons who have that power. When the sovereign lays down a rule, those under her power have an obligation to abide by that rule. But "there's the rub."

What kind of an "obligation" is that? asks H. L. A. Hart (1961, pp. 79–88). It does not follow from our *being obliged* to act from fear of the sovereign that we *have an obligation* to act. If that were so, then it would follow that, when a man obliges us to part with our money at the point of a gun, we have an obligation to give him our money. Hart protests that, on Austin's account, our relation to the sovereign, and hence to the law, is no different from our relation to the gunman. There is no room for obligation in any such account (Hart, 1961, Ch. II). Still, how, on Hart's analysis, are we to distinguish between laws that are and those that are not morally obligatory? Hart offers a more sophisticated definition of law than his positivist predecessor. Law, Hart tells us, consists of more than the prohibitions and requirements on which Austin's analysis focuses. These are, in Hart's terminology, primary rules. But a legal system composed entirely of such rules would be inadequate on several counts. We would have no way of determining what the rules are or the scope of a given rule; there would be no way to change the rules as conditions change; and such a system would lack an authoritative and final determination that a rule had been violated. To avoid these deficiencies, a viable legal system will contain, besides primary rules, three kinds of secondary rules: rules of recognition, change, and adjudication (Hart, 1961, Ch. V).

As Hart and other critics of Austin continue to insist, we do feel some obligation to abide by the law, but the positivist account of obligation is unsatisfactory. What can account for that feeling? Or is it simply mistaken to feel that way? Is it, perhaps, the residue of an out-of-date notion that just because someone or some group, like the king or the feudal barons of old, holds power over us we owe him or them fealty? At most, that would explain our having such a feeling, but it would not justify it.

In fact, it is not even an accurate explanation because fealty to a lord or the king was, at least ideally, a reciprocal matter. It was not *only* because the king or lord had the power to compel us that we owed him obedience but also that he was responsible for our well-being. He was, for that reason, not like the gunman demanding our wallet. His responsibilities toward us were matched by our responsibilities to abide by the rules he laid down for our governance. Depending on how seriously those responsibilities were taken on both sides, there could be a quite understandable sense that one had an obligation to obey the law.

But how can there be an obligation to obey *all* laws? Isn't it notoriously true that there are and have been a great many morally questionable laws? In the all-too-recent history of the United States, there have been laws requiring the return of an escaped slave or prohibiting the marriage of a Black to a White. In South Africa today, there are laws that bolster the policy of apartheid. In Hitler's Germany (and no doubt in many other totalitarian states), there were laws that required one to report to the authorities antigovernment utterances even of one's own family. Austin has overreached in attempting to find a universal obligation to obey the law. But, then, how are we to distinguish the laws that do impose obligation from those that do not? We can no longer rely on a merely formal criterion such as that the law has been enacted by a duly constituted legislature. Even well-intentioned legislatures make errors and enact laws for which there may be good moral reason to disobey.

It won't do, either, to turn, as some American jurisprudents have done, to the decisions of judges. Oliver Wendell Holmes, Jr., tells us that

> the prophecies of what the courts will do in fact, and nothing more pretentious, are what I mean by the law . . . a legal duty so-called is nothing but a prediction that if a man does or omits certain things he will be made to suffer in this or that way by judgment of the court — and so of a legal right. (Golding, p. 176)

But if legislators can make morally disreputable laws, it is equally true that judges can make morally bad decisions. Indeed, Holmes and other so-called realists are close to an important truth. Bishop Benjamin Hoadly is reported to have said (in a sermon preached before the king in 1717) that "whoever hath an *absolute authority* to *interpret* any written or spoken laws, it is *he* who is truly the *Law-giver* to all intents and purposes, and not the person who first wrote or spoke them" (as quoted by John Chipman Gray, Golding, p. 195).

Whatever lawmakers may order written then in the "black letter" of the statute books, it is the judges who must decide how those requirements are to be applied to the cases that come before them. In a constitutional system of law, the judges —

or those judges who are justices of a state or of the federal Supreme Court — have even more power because they may decide whether the legislature's enactment is legally valid.

But there is something unsatisfactory in these legal positivist and legal realist positions. We are searching for the source of the obligation to abide by the law, and we do not seem even to have come near it. What we have found, at best, is a criterion of what is to count as a law. A rule is a law if, and only if, it is duly enacted by a legislature or if, and only if, it can be predicted confidently that the courts will enforce it. Why should we suppose that we have an obligation to do what the legislature or the courts require? Legislatures and courts can impose all sorts of foolish and wicked requirements. Is there a way to set off the rules that are morally obligatory from those that, even though they may be enacted and enforced, are not obligatory?

The legal positivists insisted, rightly, that it is important to distinguish the question "What is a law?" from the question "What is a good law?" ". . . [P]ositive law (or law, simply and strictly so called)," Austin tells us, "is often confounded . . . with objects which are also signified, properly and improperly, by the large and vague expression *law*" (Golding, p. 77). Many people use "law" in an honorific sense, to apply only to rules that they believe have been laid down by God or that conscience tells them should be obeyed. To this, Austin replies, with grim humor:

> . . . . [T]o say that human laws which conflict with the Divine law are not binding, that is to say, are not laws, is to talk stark nonsense. The most pernicious laws, and therefore those which are most opposed to the will of God, have been and are continually enforced as laws by judicial tribunals. Suppose an act innocuous, or positively beneficial, be prohibited by the sovereign under the penalty of death; if I commit this act, I shall be tried and condemned, and if I object to the sentence, that it is contrary to the law of God, who has commanded that human lawgivers shall not prohibit acts which have no evil consequences, the Court of Justice will demonstrate the inconclusiveness of my reasoning by hanging me up, in pursuance of the law of which I have denied the validity. (Golding, pp. 96–97)

If Austin rates high marks for analytic sharpness, in passages such as this one, does he not also exhibit a less-than-admirable moral obtuseness? Indeed, we should clear our heads about what constitutes legal validity. A law is a law even if it is a bad law. But Austin *seems* not to recognize the source of our unease with his insistence on giving pride of place ("law simply and strictly so called") to positive law. We are not satisfied with an account that seems to translate questions about the moral acceptability of a law into questions about the law's legal validity. We don't want to know whether the law that requires the return of a slave to her "rightful owner" is appropriately enacted and predictably enforced, but whether in conscience it can be obeyed. The moral of Austin's analysis is that we should not couch our qualms about the moral obligatoriness of a law in the form of a question whether that (legally valid) law *is* a law. So far, so good, but how then can we distinguish morally unacceptable laws from those that we can in conscience obey?

Austin has an answer to that question that may not be apparent to the reader who is unaware that Austin (along with most of the other legal positivists) is an ardent supporter of the utilitarian movement. Good laws are those that are in the interest of the greatest happiness of the greatest number of people. Bad laws have consequences that are on the whole more likely to create misery than happiness. But the utilitarian position is not that each citizen should do a quick calculation whether the consequences of a law are on the whole good or bad, on each occasion when he falls under a legal requirement. The consequences of *that* practice would likely be the undermining of the force of law. Rather, if law is to serve to regulate conduct in a way that is for the greatest happiness, then there must be a taken-for-granted presumption that a valid law should be obeyed. Except in the most extreme circumstances, those in which a thoroughly evil regime is in power, the burden of moral proof will lie on her who would disobey a valid law.

If we were to pursue this topic further, we would have to distinguish, as Kent Greenawalt does, between laws that serve primarily to regulate conduct and those that serve mainly to keep a government in power (Greenawalt, Ch. 4). Laws that regulate conduct may be morally obligatory even if legislated and enforced by an evil regime — given that the alternative of a nonregulated, and hence chaotic, condition is not acceptable. Laws that serve to keep a government in power *may* be acceptable, even if they are laws of an evil regime because the alternative could be an even more evil regime or anarchy. The ordinary run of criminal laws, laws that in slightly differing forms are to be found in every complex society, is what is primarily at issue here: laws against indiscriminate killing, assault, rape, and robbery, for example. We can't do without them; and to undercut them by encouraging disobedience to them or to hamstring any government's ability to enforce them is morally dubious.

NATURAL LAW

The natural law position, in legal philosophy and ethics, is the expression of the concern that there must be some substantive basis for the moral assessment of rules. There are all kinds of rules, some worthy of allegiance and obedience, some not. How are we to distinguish the worthy from the unworthy, the true from the false, the authoritative from the sham-authoritative? St. Thomas Aquinas (1225–1274), in the *Summa Theologica*, will not accept as an answer that "whatsoever pleases the sovereign has the force of *law*." For a rule to count as *law*, not merely as the law the ruler lays down, it must derive from reason — from premises that are rock-solid, fundamental, undeniable. *Law* is morally binding, not merely decreed and enforced. It is therefore true by definition that a *law* binds conscience, is not to be obeyed merely because a government has the power to enforce it.

Where is this reason to be found that will yield us *law?* What is the *law* that it yields? Reason is a faculty that is innate in humans, having been instilled in us by God; it distinguishes us from the rest of the animal kingdom. Aquinas apparently considers all acceptable reasoning to be deductive in nature. A deductive argument is valid if the conclusion follows from the premises. If the argument starts from false premises, then it may be valid but the conclusion still false. A deductive argument must, if it is to yield consistently true conclusions, be not only valid but sound. A sound argument is one that is valid and begins from true premises.

Reason must therefore yield us true beginning premises, indisputably true ones, if we are to trust our conclusions concerning the content of *law.* How can a premise be indisputably true? Is there any proposition at all that may not somewhere, sometime turn out to be false? If grass is green on this planet, may it not be red if cultivated on Mars? If all swans so far discovered are white, may it still not be false (as it so turned out) that all swans are white? But there is a class of propositions that do seem immune to this sort of contingency: self-evident propositions. A self-evident proposition's "predicate is contained in the notion of the subject." In modern terms, it is analytic; its truth follows from the very meaning of the words it uses. There are trivial analytic truths that may serve us as stalking horses for apparently more weighty ones. For example, it is analytically, or self-evidently, true that a cube has twelve edges.

That example, which could be multiplied into thousands, has an advantage, for our purposes, over even simpler examples such as that all bachelors are unmarried or that vixens are foxes. It is that the claim that cubes have twelve edges may not at first be apparent; we have to think about it to realize that it is true. More complicated mathematical truths would require more reflection than that one. But the point is that, even though a proposition is self-evidently true, we may not at first, or for a long time, or perhaps ever recognize its self-evidence. To use Aquinas's language, it may be self-evident in itself, even if it is not self-evident in relation to us. To speak metaphorically, it is as if God has placed certain truths deep within our minds and has given us the tool, reason, with which to probe for them. But not all of us will take the trouble to use the tool, and some of us will never develop the capacity to use it well.

Still, if we are to discover *law,* we must start from self-evident truths. Mathematical examples are not useful. Where are we to begin? Aquinas offers, as "the first principle in the practical reason . . . one founded on the nature of good, viz., that *good is that which all things seek after.*" Hence, he tells us, the first precept of law is that "*good is to be done and promoted, and evil is to be avoided.*" All other precepts of natural law, he says, are based on this one, "so that all the things which the practical reason naturally apprehends as man's good belong to the precepts of the natural law under the form of things to be done or avoided" (Golding, p. 18).

The idea seems to be that, given the reason that God has implanted in us, we can see what is good and evil for us, individually and collectively—and the principle tells us that we should pursue good and avoid evil. But first, before reason, we have natural instincts in common with other animals. Specifically, we have the instinct of self-preservation. It is therefore a part of natural law that we do what we can to preserve our own lives. No life, no pursuit of good. Then the reason that is a part of our human nature leads us to the pursuit of good.

What is good? Natural reason tells us,

> Man has a natural inclination to know the truth about God, and to live in society; and in this respect, whatever pertains to this inclination belongs to the natural law: e.g., to shun ignorance, to avoid offending those among whom one has to live, and other such things regarding the above inclination. (Golding, p. 19)

These general (and very vague) principles are unchanging, but the particular human laws that are derived from them may vary according to the circumstances of different peoples in different places and times.

This last proviso might seem to go a certain distance toward reassuring Jeremy Bentham against the arbitrariness of appeals to natural law. Bentham, noting widespread disagreement about the content of natural law, characterized natural law as one of the forms of the pseudoprinciple of sympathy and antipathy. That principle, remember, is that what is eternally right is what the speaker likes and what is always and everywhere wrong is what he dislikes. The proviso at least accounts for there being different opinions concerning what the natural law demands because the same general principles may demand different laws for different circumstances. But still, would Bentham and Austin, and do we, have reason to accept the natural law position? There are several reasons why they and we might be reluctant to do so.

CRITICISMS OF THE NATURAL LAW POSITION

The first difficulty is with Aquinas's notion of the good. He assumes without argument a "teleology" he inherits from Aristotle: All of nature, including humankind, has some good toward which it strives. We are, on this theory, naturally end-seekers, and each kind of being has its own peculiar end, its good. This seems plausible when we speak of plants and lower animals. The end of a tomato plant is to produce tomatoes. To that purpose, it must root itself in good soil and reach toward the sun. The end of a mussel is to grow to juicy maturity; it must therefore attach itself to an intertidal rock and filter nutrients out of seawater. However, it is less than clear when applied to humans and even to the higher animals. What is the good of Sam, my Labrador retriever? What is my good? Sam no doubt wants to survive, as do I. Survival is a condition of achieving whatever good is appropriate to each of us. But (to leave Sam) what *is* my good? I must know what it is if I am to know what laws are *laws*, derivable from natural law. It is not clear that there is any such good. The assumption that there is one needs argument, argument that has in the long history of natural law theory not been satisfactorily forthcoming.

Second, even if I could understand my own good on some extended analogy with the good of the tomato plant and the mussel, I would still not be in position to say what laws there should be because what good the laws are designed to preserve is not only mine but a collective one, the community's good. It is notorious that there are different conceptions of a good community, just as there are conflicting ideals of personal development. The Athenians had very different communal ideals from the Spartans, the Iranians from the Americans, and the Indians from the Chinese. It does not follow, of course, that because there are inconsistent conceptions of communal good there is not some true conception. But if there is one, Aquinas's vague indications are less than helpful in locating it.

The vagueness of the natural law position seems endemic. To offer natural laws that are at all specific is to encourage the charge that there is no consensus about the content of natural law. What is sure and beyond question must then be principles that are more abstract and general. But principles as abstract and general as those Aquinas lists are consistent with radically different conceptions of the good for man.

Third, there is the problem that, in retreating to self-evident principles, we sacrifice relevance to the problems of legislation. If a proposition is true merely because of the meaning of the words in which it is formulated, it would seem that it is merely a proposition *about* the words. It is unshakably true that "girls are female children," but that tells us nothing about how girls should conduct their lives—unless we presuppose non-self-evident rules about how children or females should live. But where does the self-evidence of natural law come from if not from assumptions about the meaning of words or (equally irrelevant to legislation) the implications of mathematical constructions?

The theological explanation that natural laws owe their self-evidence to their having been placed in our minds by God does not help because self-evidence is the criterion of their having been so placed. We are supposed to know *from* their self-evidence that God placed them there. Mere common sense won't do as a criterion of self-evidence. What is the merest common sense of one age and place may be rank lunacy in another.

It seems inescapable that advocates of natural law must rely on intuition as the source of their knowledge of the beginning principles of law. Reason determines the content of natural law by intuition of what is already present in the mind. But once we move beyond mathematical and merely verbal truths, we are in the realm of controversy. People's intuitions differ. Alf Ross asks,

> Is it nature's bidding that men shall be as brothers, or is it nature's law that the strong shall rule over the weak, and that therefore slavery and class distinctions are part of God's meaning for the world? Both propositions have been asserted

with the same support and the same "right"; for how should anyone be able to make a choice between these absolutes except by an absolute assertion elevated above all rational argumentation: It is so because I know that it is so! The ideology of equality was preached by the Sophists in the fifth century B.C. and by Rousseau in the eighteenth century. . . . Plato, on the other hand, postulated the innate inequality of men, and advocated slavery and a community strictly divided into classes. Aristotle followed him with regard to the natural justification of slavery, and since then the postulate concerning the natural inequality of men has been the point of departure for many conservative doctrines of natural law and organic or totalitarian theories of government. (Golding, pp. 69–70)

Finally, there is the problem of exactly how natural law is itself morally obligatory and transmits that obligatoriness to the laws that are supposedly derived from it. When we are told that a bill in Congress has been enacted into law, we know that we disobey it on pain of suffering the penalty that is attached. We have a motive of prudence for obeying it. If we are told that the newly enacted law is also derivable from natural law, do we thereby incur a new motive to obey it, a moral obligation? How does this come about? It will not do to say that the natural law from which the newly enacted law is derived is self-evident. That tells us at most that we may be sure that it *is* a natural law. But why do we have a moral obligation to do what natural law requires? We cannot presuppose the theological position that we have an obligation because the natural law is God's command. Its being commanded by God rests, apparently, on its being self-evident. But the self-evident propositions of which we have found examples are not commands at all. What would a self-evident *command* look like? More important, why does God command it? Presumably because it is what we ought to do. But why ought we to do what it requires? Because it is self-evident. We are in a circle.

SOME SUPPOSED ROLES OF LAW

We have been approaching the problem of the distinction between and the relation of law and morality by speaking of theories of the nature of law. That has not been a satisfactory move, although both the positivist–realist theory and natural law theory do articulate commonly held and seemingly commonsense notions. On the one hand, law must be defined in such a way that we can speak meaningfully of there being good and bad laws. We should not reserve the title *law* only for good laws. That is confusing. On the other hand, if law is to command respect, a sense of obligation, it must rest on undeniably obligatory principles. If the attempt to define law has not been a success, an approach from the other direction — defining morality — might be more useful. Supposing that we could arrive at a suitable definition of morality, then legal rules might be definable by contrast with moral ones. That will be the approach of the next chapter. But before turning to the question of the definition of morality, we should notice some of the *roles* that have been assigned to law as a means of distinguishing it from morality.

It is not unusual to think of law as the shield, or protector, of morality. By enforcing moral rules, law prevents the backsliding and moral decay that are threats to the existence of any given social order. If stealing, assault, and murder were permitted without penalty, the moral disapproval that attaches to those actions would not be enough to prevent them. By curbing the excesses of the pornographic industry and by limiting the violence on the TV screen, law challenges antisocial, immoral conceptions of what is and is not permissible in human relations. This conception of the role of law presupposes that "morality" is univocal, that it refers to some one set of prohibitions and requirements, to some unique underlying principles, or to some particular pattern of approved qualities of character. That presupposition, as we will see in the next chapter, is open to question. Still, there is a wide consensus that certain acts prohibited by criminal law are morally wrong, that legally enforceable duties arising out of contract are often morally required, and that there are dissolute and dangerous qualities of character that legal regulation of the media may help minimize.

The danger in this conception of law is that there is a smooth path between it and "paternalism": excessive interference of government with the right of adult human beings to chart their own lives, to decide what they may and may not do, read, see or experience. We will notice the debate over paternalism in Chapter 12.

It is sometimes said (for example, by Justice Holmes) that the proper role of law is to control external behavior, whereas the appropriate task of morality is to govern by means of internal motive. Although this view of the appropriate roles of law and morality seems close to the mark, it requires clarification and qualification. We will consider it in Chapter 10.

CONCLUSION

The conclusions of this chapter are simply stated. The insistence of the legal positivists and legal realists on distinguishing the question what the law *is* from the question what it *ought to be* is well justified. To argue, as the natural law advocates do, that true law (*law*) must be derivable from the principles of natural law, is to confuse the moral acceptability of a law with its legal bindingness. On the other hand, legal positivists and (especially) legal realists *seem* not to give proper weight to the question how morally acceptable laws are to be distinguished from unacceptable ones. This apparent failure of moral acuteness may result from the assumption, at least on the part of Austin, of an underlying, but not explicitly employed, criterion of moral acceptability: the utilitarian theory. Whether that theory is itself acceptable, we have not discussed. It is too controverted and complex an issue to take up in this book. We have found that it does not, by itself, provide an acceptable justification of legal punishment.

Natural law theory, in Aquinas's presentation of it, confuses the question of what is to count as law and the question of what is morally binding law. It rightly seeks some criterion by which we can distinguish with assurance morally obligatory law from law that is not obligatory. But the criterion offered suffers serious defects. Its claim to provide a rock-solid foundation for law turns out to rest on the assurance with which we can accept analytic judgments. However, the judgment from which Aquinas begins turns out not to be analytic but to rest on the questionable assumption that there is some good peculiar to people. If it were analytic, there would remain the question of how analytic propositions can ground claims about the moral obligatoriness of law.

Morality as a Code of Rules

What is the "morality" with which law is to be contrasted? The term is notoriously ambiguous. *Morality* can refer to the moral beliefs of a given community, the justified moral beliefs of a community, moral beliefs (if any) that are universally held, or to justified universally held moral beliefs. In addition, there is the question of what kind of thing the beliefs are about. A frequent candidate is moral rules. The notion is that questions of moral right and wrong—rights, duties, and obligations—arise in a way parallel to questions of law. To find answers, we must have recourse to rules, to the moral rules by reference to which particular cases can be decided. The rules themselves must, if they can be justified at all, be justified by reference to a set of moral principles (Fried, Ch. 1; Gert, Chs. 1 and 8).

MORAL RULES

Given this understanding of morality, the question how moral questions are to be distinguished from legal ones translates into a jurisdictional query: Under which set of rules, moral or legal, does the case fall? If we could be clear about the distinguishing characteristics of moral rules, perhaps we could then more easily draw the boundaries between the legal and moral realms.

The most commonly offered example of a moral rule is that promises ought to be kept. If the promise in question is also a legal contract, then a moral and a legal rule may have convergent effects: There is both a moral and a legal obligation to do what one has engaged to do. Swinburne has promised Rosetti to sell him her house; they have signed a legally valid contract giving Rosetti an option to buy the house; Rosetti brings a certified check for the proper amount. Swinburne's daughter now decides she would like her mother to keep the house. Should she do so? There seem to be conclusive grounds, moral and legal, for her not keeping it.

By stipulating that the contract was legally valid, we rule out such exceptions as that Swinburne had been coerced to sign it or that she had been insane at the time she signed the contract. But there could be conflicting legal obligations. Swinburne might have signed an equally valid contract giving Jonson an option to buy or the municipality might claim the house under eminent domain. If the legal contract is to be binding, we must not only say that it is valid but that there are no conflicting or overriding legal obligations.

The moral obligation seems to be in this respect quite parallel to the legal one. That is, the promise Swinburne made to Rosetti is not a valid one if someone had coerced Swinburne to make such a promise or if she had been insane at the time that she made it. There might have been conflicting moral obligations. She might also have validly promised the house to Spenser. It might turn out that, because someone else takes the house away from her, she can no longer fulfill her promise. What then, if anything, distinguishes the legal from the moral obligation? The characteristic most often mentioned is that legal obligations are *enforceable*; moral obligations are not. Swinburne must fulfill her legal obligations or suffer economic penalties or imprisonment. No consequences of this kind follow her breaking a promise; still there may well be consequences.

What kinds of consequences? Is it here, in the difference of consequences for violation, that we will find a distinction between moral and legal rules? What happens if Swinburne breaks her promise to Rosetti?

Rosetti may avoid Swinburne in the future.

Rosetti may shame Swinburne by making public Swinburne's promise breaking.

Rosetti may try to get even, take vengeance.

Rosetti's relatives and friends may shun Swinburne.

Swinburne's friends and the people with whom she does or would like to do business may no longer trust her promises or assurances.

A common characteristic of these responses is that it would be impractical or impossible to accommodate them in a legal system—to transform them into legal responses. Why should promisees be legally required to avoid promise breakers? Where is the legal line to be drawn between the breaking of a trivial and a significant promise? How could there be legal proceedings turning on a verbal assurance made in the absence of witnesses? What would ensure, in the absence of procedures for verifying that a promise had been made, that there would not be false claims that there had been a promise? How do we define the legal "penalties" of shunning and distrusting in such a way that people can know in any clear way what the law requires of them?

Are we to define moral rules residually then as rules that cannot easily (or at all) be brought under a legal system? That will not do. The domain of rules extends further than the combination of legal and moral rules. For example, there are rules of navigation, architectural design, and chess. In fact, the concept of a rule is an expansible duffel bag containing very many different items. It is not clear that those items have any single characteristic in common. Some rules, like the rules of chess, determine what it is to engage in a practice. (It has been remarked that you cannot play *chess* without the queen.) Other rules, like the rules of architectural design, often amount to guidelines, hints, helpful reminders. The rules of celestial navigation are formulas that will, if followed, determine beyond reasonable question the latitude and longitude of a ship or plane. The tactical rules of chess, as opposed to the rules of the game governing what may be done with each piece, resemble those rules of architecture that serve as guides to successful design. The rules of navigation—for example, the rules by which we can determine latitude from the altitude of a star—are somewhat like tactical rules or the rules for design in that they are guidelines to a successful outcome. They differ in that it can be shown, demonstrated, that they lead to the desired result, the establishment of a position.

If moral rules cannot be defined as nonlegal rules, do they have some common, nonresidual characteristic? Here we run into a problem. Moral rules are not, as a class, like the classes of trees, hedges, or grass. Although there will be borderline cases in the latter classes—such as tall shrubs, naturally growing bushy borders, and vinelike ground cover—there is also universal agreement over a wide range of examples what is to count as a tree, a hedge, or grass. By contrast, the list of moral rules over which there is universal agreement is, to say the least, short. It becomes increasingly problematic what is to be included as we move beyond the rule that promises should be kept.

MORAL PRINCIPLES

In fact, two different sorts of example come to mind. On the one hand, there are rules that parallel the rules of criminal law, such as the prohibition of assault, robbery, and murder. The promise-keeping rule is parallel to the law of contracts. The rule that we should not intentionally damage others' property parallels the law of torts. On the other hand, there are much more abstract (and necessarily vague) rules, perhaps better called principles. Here are some examples:

Treat others as you would be treated (The Golden Rule).

Treat relevantly like cases alike and relevantly different cases differently (a Principle of Justice).

Do not do what would be wrong if it were generally done (The Universalization Principle).

Do what is for the greatest happiness of the greatest happiness of the greatest number (The Utilitarian Principle).

Although there are points of divergence, this second category, that of principles, seems also to find a parallel to or an identity with legal principles. The principle that like cases should be treated alike provides the closest parallel. It is inherent in the principle of the rule of law. *Ideally*, under a legal system, a duly enacted law or the common law will be applied to everyone in the same way. It will not matter that a given lawbreaker is a relative of the judge or that he comes from an important family. We will not find one person serving a life sentence while the sentence that another serves for the same crime in the same circumstances is six months. The rule of law is opposed to the rule of men; under the latter system there are no constraints on partial or prejudiced interpretations of legal rules. Rules become mere commands, commands that may apply only to those in special disfavor.

The principle that we should not do what would be wrong if generally done could serve as a guideline for those who, because they are legislators, must ask what laws are and are not desirable. In this guise, the principle says to restrict legal prohibitions to those that cover acts that, if generally done, would be collectively harmful. The prohibition of littering, discharging raw sewage, or vending on crowded sidewalks can serve as examples. Similarly, the moral principle that we should consider the happiness of everyone concerned can, as we have seen in our discussion of punishment, serve equally well as a principle of legislation and adjudication.

If the principle that we should treat others as we would be treated seems least like a legal principle, that may be because it points less markedly toward a specific sort of legislation or adjudication. On the other hand, it would be hard to deny the relevance of such a principle in legislative debate or in arguments before the bench about the way in which a bill should be enacted or a law interpreted and applied.

A somewhat different but equally fundamental principle, attributable to Immanuel Kant, is that we should never treat persons, including ourselves, as a mere means to some end but always as ends in themselves (Kant, 1785, Ch. 2). This obscure but important notion is often referred to as the Principle of Respect. It is easier to grasp in its negative formulation than in its positive one. To treat a person as a mere means is to *use* her. It is to fail to see that, as a separate person and a member of the community, *her* interests, feelings, aims must be weighed if she is to be affected by the law or decision. The principle applies even if it be conceded that the proposed legislation or judicial decision would be for the collective good of everyone concerned. Individuals are not to be used even for the attainment of the general happiness or the avoidance of general misery.

INTEGRITY: A MORAL PRINCIPLE?

Ronald Dworkin, a contemporary legal philosopher, argues for a conception of political community that is informed by the Principle of Integrity. That principle holds, with respect to adjudication, that judges should found their decisions on as coherent an account as they can muster of the underlying principles of the legal system of which they are officials:

> Integrity demands that the public standards of the community be both made and seen, so far as this is possible, to express a single, coherent scheme of justice and fairness in the right relation. An institution that accepts that ideal will sometimes, for that reason, depart from a narrow line of past decisions in search of fidelity to principles conceived as more fundamental to the scheme as a whole. (p. 219)

Dworkin has in mind here more than mere consistency in legislation and adjudication. The principled approach to law requires a certain conception of a political community, one characterized by what Dworkin calls the Model of Principle. This model

> . . . insists that people are members of a genuine political community only when they accept that their fates are linked in the following strong way: they accept that they are governed by common principles, not just by rules hammered out in political compromise. . . . Members of a society of principle accept that their political rights and duties are not exhausted by the particular decisions their political institutions have reached, but depend, more generally, on the scheme of principles those decisions presuppose and endorse. (p. 211)

Interestingly, Dworkin leaves open the possibility that a member of the community may not "wholeheartedly approve" of the scheme of principles. He need only accept that there are rights and duties that flow from the scheme. The obligations generated by the scheme

> arise from the historical fact that his community has adopted that scheme, which is then special to it, not the assumption that he would have chosen it were the choice entirely his. In short, each accepts political integrity as a distinct political ideal and treats the general acceptance of that ideal, even among people who otherwise disagree about political morality, as constitutive of political community. (p. 211)

What Dworkin seems to have in mind is that people can disagree about what justice or fairness require and still feel bound by the consensus of the community as expressed in the institutions that have built up over time. What Dworkin does not envision is that integrity requires agreement over principles that are morally repugnant. In fact, integrity can be understood two ways. It can be the simple requirement that, if there is to be a political community at all, there must be general agreement on the principles that underlie legislation and adjudication. On that understanding, there could be a morally evil community none of whose principles would be morally acceptable, but which principles are nevertheless knit into a coherent scheme of governance. Or integrity can be a necessary condition of a morally acceptable conception of community in which, even though there are differences of interpretation of the key terms, everyone is committed to justice and fairness in the law.

Understood in this latter way, integrity is what we might call a second-level principle. It is moral not because of its efficacy in holding a community together, but because it presupposes moral notions—even though there may be different interpretations of those notions within an integral community. It presupposes that the community that is to be sustained is moral.

NORMATIVE AND DESCRIPTIVE MORALITY

In asking what morality is and how it can be contrasted to law, a distinction must be made that interestingly parallels distinctions we have already discovered in discussions of the nature of law. We can speak of the rules and principles that a people in fact hold as their morality. Colin Wilson can report that it is a part of the morality of the mountain people of a certain section of Africa that each person looks out for himself, that he has no great concern for the welfare of his family, to say nothing of the welfare of the community at large. This is to speak descriptively, to report what others believe and practice. Normatively, on the other hand, we can ask whether the rules and principles of the mountain people are moral (morally acceptable) ones. Failure to insist on the distinction between normative and descriptive morality could confuse our pursuit of an answer to the question what that elusive "morality" is which is to be contrasted with law.

The distinction between normative and descriptive might also have been applied to theories of the nature of law, but we would not have wanted to apply the distinction at the risk of begging questions. While it seemed that what positivists and realists had in mind was a descriptive account, still when John Austin or Oliver Wendell Holmes, Jr., insist that law is nothing more than the command of the sovereign or the interpretation of judges, they seem to be insisting that we ought to call law only what fits those descriptions. Is this to introduce a normative element in their account of law? I think not. The normativity of their claims and contentions has to do not with what ought to be law, but with what is the best description of law. Admittedly, there is yet another normative element in at least the realistic theory. Holmes's famous address, from which we have quoted, was delivered to law students at Harvard. Given the context, Holmes can and perhaps should be read as telling prospective lawyers that they would do well not to be confused by natural law and other theories concerning law. Their business is to find out what the law is for their clients, and the place to look for law is in judicial decisions. They ought to seek it there. But this is still not a theory about what the law ought to be, but about where it is to be found.

Natural law theorists, on the other hand, might have reason to reject any sharp distinction between normative and descriptive accounts of law. There is no reason why an Aquinas need deny the usefulness of a purely descriptive account of legal codes. Nevertheless, "law" does assume an honorific, approbative sense in his theory. *Law*, true law, is derivable from self-evident principles instilled in the human mind by God. That is the law that ought to be obeyed; and human law is obligatory only to the degree that it can be reconciled with *law*.

Descriptively speaking then, there can be both legal and moral codes of which we morally disapprove. Our several problems about the relation of law and morality, mentioned at the beginning of this chapter, have to do not with "our morality" as one code among many possible ones, but with a code and principles that we accept, to which we are committed. Our primary commitment is to the moral principles on which the code rests. Moral codes, like laws, may have to change to accommodate new ideas and new circumstances. Right or wrong, we think of the principles, to which we appeal in arguing for change, as themselves not changeable. For example, however remiss we may be in following it, we would not easily give up the principle that we should treat others as we would have them treat us.

A rule is moral then, normatively speaking, if it rests on normatively moral principles. What are these principles? I simply stipulate, for present purposes and without claiming comprehensiveness, that the principles I have listed in this chapter are moral. I do not try to show that these and only these principles are the solid ground on which codes suitable to the factual circumstances of different times and places should be erected. I do not believe that they are the only moral principles worthy of acceptance, but I do believe that they are worthy.

Moral codes, justifiable by reference to our principles, can be coincident with legal codes. They may permit or prohibit much the same things as criminal or contract law does. Still, there are morally wrong acts for which there may be good reason *not* to prohibit as a matter of law. They may be unenforceable, or difficult to enforce, or the attempt to enforce them may have adverse consequences for the system of law as a whole. For example, it is morally wrong not to be sensitive to another's suffering, not to care about it. It is a sign of a person's moral incompleteness that he fails to feel what he should in the presence of suffering. But how to enact a law requiring people to feel for sufferers? Even if such a law were draftable, were enacted, were enforceable, and did not adversely affect the system of law as a whole, it would affect the common moral life. It would, just because it is now an enforceable duty, cast into question the motives a person may have for doing the things and saying the things that a sympathetic person would do or say. What is morally required is that she be sympathetic, that she have the motive of sympathy. It is difficult to understand how a person could be legally required to have that motive.

SECOND THOUGHTS ABOUT MORALITY AS A CODE OF RULES

Earlier in this chapter, we wondered how full and rich a list of moral rules might be, observing that it is not easy to move in a noncontroversial way far beyond the rule that promises ought to be kept. Nevertheless, we then went on to suppose that there are moral rules parallel to a good many rules of law. For example, we said that there are moral as well as legal rules against murder, robbery, and the intentional damage of another's property. This line of thought can generate a picture of morality as consisting of a kind of shadow law, a quasi-legal code that is in important respects weaker than law. There are no institutions for the code's enforcement: no published prohibitions and requirements; no judges, juries, or jailers. It must be enforced, if at all, informally. Furthermore, there is no established mechanism, as there is in law, for adding to, subtracting from, or otherwise changing the code. They suffer, in short, from the defects that H. L. A. Hart identifies as failings of a pure system of primary rules, defects that cannot, in the nature of the case, be corrected by the addition of secondary rules of recognition, change, and adjudication.

On this view of law and morality, law's business is to stiffen morality's spine. Morality pre-exists law, and the function of law is to give it force. But there is something uncomfortably artificial about all of this. We are speaking about a code, the moral code, that is unwritten, has undefined boundaries, and is open to differing versions. Suppose the pictures were reversed? Why should the legal code not be primary, as a necessity of human social order? Can we easily imagine a social order without enforced rules? Why should not the idea that there is a moral code arise because there are rules that we might like to incorporate in a legal code but that we cannot or should not enforce for practical reasons—like the rule about being sympathetic? Perhaps legal *and* moral rules are rules deemed necessary or desirable for communal life, and moral rules *are*, within *that* category, the residual class of rules for which there is no institutional mechanism of enactment, judicial application to particular cases, or enforcement by the threat of punishment.

This would seem to relegate moral rules to a less central role than legal rules. But it is important to note two matters. The first is that moral *principles* may still be fundamentally important in the evaluation of legal systems. To be committed to a legal system (as opposed to a system of the commands of a sovereign who is capable of enforcing them), is to be committed to the Rule of Law. It is an implication of the Rule of Law that relevantly like cases are to be treated alike and relevantly different cases differently. There is therefore at least one moral principle that underlies the very ideal of a system of law. What about the three other formulations I have stipulated as moral principles? The universalization principle and the utilitarian principle (whether or not the former is a special case of the latter) set a standard, however abstract, that serves to distinguish morally acceptable from morally unacceptable systems of law. A system that did not premise legal prohibitions on the undesirability of patterns of action or that did not take into account the good of persons affected by proposed legislation would be for those reasons morally questionable.

The second matter that we should note is this: Our objective in this chapter has been to achieve an understanding of morality that would allow its contrast with law and might provide at least the beginning of answers to the questions with which we began the chapter. Our assumption, for the purpose of the discussion in this chapter, has been that morality can be encompassed in rules and principles. But is that a satisfactory conception of morality? What are we leaving out? Can morality be so narrowly understood? In Chapter 10, we will argue that it cannot. Rules and the principles that support them concern what is or is not permissible, or what we are required, to *do*. Yet morality is also intimately concerned with what persons should *be*—with qualities of character. What are the kinships and differences between the law–morality relationship and that between doing and being?

| CONCLUSION

In this chapter, we have searched for a way of distinguishing between law and morality in which each realm is conceived to be one of rules. This has led us to an uncomfortable conclusion: The province of morality may be a handmaiden to law. Moral rules may be nothing but rules necessary or desirable for communal life that, for practical reasons, we cannot or should not enact into law. At the same time, we noted that, if we search for the most general and abstract moral principles, we seem to find principles that can serve also for the moral criticism of law. What is legally valid—that is, duly and properly enacted and enforced—may at the same time not measure up to the requirements of one of the principles we have recognized, for example, the utilitarian principle. Finally, we wondered whether, in thinking of morality as a set of rules and principles concerning what we ought or ought not to do, we had not chosen too narrow a criterion. Commonsensically, morality certainly seems to be as much concerned with what kind of persons we ought to be as with what in particular we should and should not do. Does this suggest a new beginning in our attempt to set off the proper concerns of morality from the legitimate province of law?

CHAPTER 10

Morality and Law: Being and Doing

Vast overlaps exist between moral and legal concerns. Very many sorts of acts are both morally and legally wrong. To whatever extent morality can be conceived as a code of rules and principles, many of the same rules, and arguably the same principles, can be found enshrined in law. How then, if at all, can we set off the "province" of morality from that of law?

Law is, whatever else it may be, a complex practice with complex subpractices and ancillary practices. These practices can be defined in terms of rules and roles. The rules, as we have seen, are not confined to the primary ones that tell us what we must, can, or cannot do. There are also secondary rules that govern the way in which a primary rule can be recognized, changed, or adjudicated. Law—understood in this way, as a union of primary and secondary rules—must also include roles: the positions under and defined by the rules, for example, the roles of plaintiff, defendant, judge, juror, legislator, lawyer, bailiff, warden, or convict.

As we have noticed, morality, too, can be thought of as a complex of rules. But moral rules lack the complexity introduced by the secondary rules, and a morality defined by primary rules suffers from the deficiencies that the secondary rules are designed to correct. Rules of recognition are a remedy for uncertainty over the question of what is and is not a rule; rules of change are a remedy for the static nature of simple primary rules; and rules of adjudication make possible authoritative determinations that a primary rule has been violated (Hart, 1961, pp. 89–91). Moral duties and obligations, in light of this comparison with legal ones, may seem to suffer a lack of definition, flexibility, and authority. They are held to be like legal rules while lacking some of the essential qualities of legal rules. To think of morality as a complex of rules is therefore to relegate it to the role of a pallid cousin of the law, one whose outlines are fuzzy and who need not be taken so seriously as law. If we are to draw a boundary between legal and moral concerns, while doing justice to the force and poignancy of moral considerations, we seem to need a more vigorous and sharply differentiated conception of morality.

This chapter therefore speculatively explores the advantages and some of the complications of an alternative way of distinguishing between moral and legal concerns. The idea to be investigated is that morality is concerned with being and law with doing. Less mysteriously, moral concerns have ultimately to do with the character of the person, with what kind of person he *is*; legal concerns have ultimately to do with the person's acts, with what kind of thing she must, can, or cannot *do*.

Of course, we do speak of acts as being morally right or wrong, and in law we are often concerned with the psychological antecedents and accompaniments of an act. But these are, on this hypothesis, not matters of ultimate concern. To say that morality is ultimately concerned with the character of the person is to say that the question of the moral quality of the act would not arise but for questions about the character of the person committing it. On the other hand, legal interest in the psychology of the person would not exist but for the need to pass judgment on his acts.

THE MORALITY OF CHARACTER

We might begin by noticing that there are very many important moral notions that do not fit comfortably under the conception of morality as a collection of rules. There are moralities of honesty, trustworthiness, fairness, kindness, consideration, and loyalty. These notions, together with others like them, can be regarded as a matrix out of which a second conception of morality emerges, a morality of character. It is arguable that considerations concerning character are not derivable from moral rules. Is the demand that we should be honest founded on some rule from which it derives its force? It is not easy to see how such a question is to be decided.

What is a morality of character? It concerns virtues and vices, but what is a virtue and what is a vice? Both of these ancient terms refer to human dispositions, or tendencies. The following are some dispositions: hesitant, conscientious, temperate, lethargic, logical, intuitive, artistic, sincere, brave, devious, weak-willed, busy, deliberate, untrustworthy, cruel, kind, melancholy, happy, intelligent, eccentric, persistent, wise, humorous, loyal, just, stingy, selfish, generous, studious.

How, on what basis, are we to pick out those dispositions that are virtues or vices? Intuitively, cruelty is a vice, and fairness is a virtue; deliberateness or humorousness could be either or neither, depending on the circumstances. Let us try a vague but potentially useful criterion: A virtue is a disposition that provides general grounds for preference. If a disposition is a virtue, then that a person has that disposition is a reason, in general, to prefer her to a person who does not have that disposition. If the disposition is a vice, then a person's having that disposition is, in general, a reason not to prefer or even to avoid her.[1]

If Marlowe is fair, then generally speaking, there is a reason to prefer Marlowe to Jonson, who is not. If Addison is cruel and Swift is not, there is a reason, in general, to prefer Swift to Addison. On the other hand, if Keats is typically deliberate or humorous, then we might be hesitant to say that there is reason to prefer him to Shelley, who is neither, because there are recurrent circumstances in which deliberateness or humorousness are vices or are neither virtues nor vices. If Keats is typically deliberate about the next move in split-second emergencies or exhibits his sense of humor mostly at funerals and other solemn occasions, we would on those grounds *not* prefer him to Shelley whose deliberateness and humorousness do not display themselves in those ways.

Because there are as many reasons for preference or avoidance as there are virtues and vices, it is unlikely that we will be able to reduce those reasons to a simple formula or to derive them from one principle. An ethics of virtue then is an ethics concerned with answers to the question, "Generally speaking, what kind of person is X?" It is a pluralistic ethics that is focused on the rich vocabulary of dispositional terms that may be used in answer to that question (Pincoffs, Ch. 5).

VIRTUE ETHICS

Many, if not most, of those terms can refer to acts as well as to persons. Not only Keats but what Keats has done can be just, kind, selfish, or cruel. A virtue-oriented ethics extends then from the moral appraisal of character to the assessment of acts as evidence of traits of character. It is the focus on character, either directly or through the character-relevant aspects of action, that distinguishes virtue ethics from an ethics concerned primarily with rules about what to do. On the latter conception, acts are morally acceptable to the degree that they abide by rules and unacceptable as they violate rules. On the former notion, that of virtue ethics, acts are morally desirable or undesirable, good or bad, because they are evidence of good or bad character.

This much can be said, in brief, for the virtue account of morality: That whatever else morality is concerned with, it is quite certainly concerned with honesty and dishonesty, fairness and unfairness, courage and cowardice—with the virtues and vices. But at least two of the currently popular types of ethical theory rest on a questionable premise. Some types presuppose the existence of a shadow–legal realm of moral rights, duties, rules, and principles; and others presuppose that all moral judgments ultimately reduce to means–end judgments and that some particular end (for example, some conception of happiness or perfection) among many contenders is the true end to which we must bend our efforts on pain of moral wrongdoing.

Whether or not a virtue-oriented conception of morality is superior, all things considered, to other sorts of theory, it does have a significant advantage when it comes to the present task — that of distinguishing the concerns proper to morality from those that are appropriate to law. In abandoning the notion that morality consists ultimately of a set of rules, we abandon the notion that morality is (or is solely) a quasi-legal realm. If we leave to law the concern with the acceptability of actions as falling under rules that the action violates or honors, morality will now have to do with actions only as they are or are not indications of good or bad character.

To put the point another way, on any rule-oriented conception of morality, the qualities of the person doing an act tend to disappear. The concern is with the rightness or wrongness of the act by reference to a set of rules or precedents. What matters, given the act and the circumstances, is whether the act is prohibited, permitted, or required. Virtue-oriented morality, on the other hand, is essentially person-oriented. While we can speak of honest or cowardly things to do, we mean that their being done is prima facie evidence of a corresponding disposition in the person who did them. Acts borrow their moral quality from the disposition of which they are evidence. If this is so, if morality *is* essentially person-oriented and legality *is* essentially concerned with acts, then we would be on the way to the distinction we want. We would have roughly sketched a line between legal and moral concerns.

DEFENSES, AGAIN

A way to expand this intuitive distinction, so that we can get a better view of it, is to focus on considerations that are common to legal and moral reasoning. There is both legal and moral interest in at least one range of concepts that seem to overlap, to indicate that moral and legal concepts cannot be neatly divided. This is the now-familiar area of defenses (Chapter 6).

If a person has done what is wrong either legally or morally, she may plead insanity, ignorance of relevant fact, coercion, mistake, or accident. Does this coincidence of pleas show then that there is a morality of law or a legality of morals that renders any attempt to distinguish between legal and moral spheres a hopeless one? I think not. What deserves notice is the force of each sort of consideration as it is put forward in legal or moral contexts. The moral question is, if our distinction is correct, "To what extent does the external act reveal the character of the person, reveal what kind of person she is?" We know that we should not jump immediately to the conclusion that it does reveal character. There may be good reason to doubt or deny it. Coercion, accident, insanity are examples of defenses against the moral assessment of a person that would follow were there no defense that shows that what *seems* to reveal a morally deficient character, a vice, in fact does not do so.

In law we are interested in the same range of excuses: for example, insanity, accident, mistake, ignorance of fact, or compulsion. But our interest in these matters is a different one. It is, to offer a global generalization, so that we can locate liability for harm in civil law or can reduce or reprobate unwanted behavior in criminal law.

Here we want to know the nature of the act because it is only acts (or omissions) of a certain description that are appropriate objects of legal control. We want to know enough about the person who did the act at the time he did it—his intentions, knowledge of fact, sanity—so that our response will be appropriate to a qualified and not merely external description of the act.

A system of law may place more or less emphasis on defenses. Under the Code of Hammurabi (Hammurabi, passim), no mention is made of the excuses or justifications that can be offered in defense—whatever the actual practice may have been in taking defenses into account. In modern law, in nearly every industrial country, defenses play a large role in legal proceedings. We might be tempted to say that, were defenses not available to us under law, courts of justice would be confined to determining whether the law had been violated and to the assignment of appropriate penalties or punishments. That, however, would be an oversimplification. Modern law often determines the presence or absence of a violation by the degree of intention or "voluntariness" that accompanies the act. What is prohibited may be the *intentional* doing of a certain act, as in first-degree murder. Thus, the very establishment in court that the forbidden act has been done requires that the presence of intention be shown. The pleas of accident or compulsion can serve to exonerate the accused, not merely to show that she is entitled to special consideration when it comes to sentencing.

A glance back at the traditional theories of punishment may help sharpen the distinction we are sketching. Legal concern extends not only to the disposition of the wrongdoer but also to the claims, actual or potential, of other people. On the retributive view, we are to give the criminal his due because others may rightly, under law, demand it. As utilitarians, we are to imprison him for the protection of others. Neither of these theories seems to be concerned primarily with the character of the criminal. The utilitarian focus on hoped-for consequences of punishment has, as we have seen, led to the criticism that, on that theory, the wrongdoer is, in a morally disreputable way, being *used* for some purpose—the deterrence of crime. This, so it was argued, was consistent even with the punishment of an innocent person, so long as the overall consequences for deterrence were predictably good.

A parallel point can, for present purposes, be made about the retributive theory. There also the issue is not the moral assessment of the wrongdoer. It is retribution for what she has done. It is not relevant under the retributive theory to say, after the commission of murder, that the murderer is, after all, a brave and loyal person. That is not what is at issue. What is at issue is that she be paid back for what she has done, not for what she is. She has done something cruel; something cruel must therefore be done to her. But what is at issue, from the point of view of virtue ethics is what we are to think of her in light of her cruel act.

To put the present claim about the proper role of moral considerations another way, they have to do with praise, blame, acceptance, repugnance, warmth, coldness, love, and hate. Moral reasoning's business (if reasoning enters into the matter at all) is, on the present view, to back these attitudes with assessments of the agent and to found the assessments on evidence. The evidence is partly in what he does, but it is also in what he says, the expressions on his face, the attitudes he habitually evinces. We want to know whether he has, absent excuses, violated someone's rights or failed to perform his duty because we want to place him in our moral universe, decide what we think of him and how to respond to him.

THE NORMATIVE ELEMENT IN SENTENCING

This attempt to distinguish what belongs to law from what is more appropriately relegated to morality is as much a normative as a descriptive one. The line that it draws through the fuzzy common ground may well seem too sharp and well defined, the respective provinces to be separated more than their overlap warrants. The account offered seems to say, for example, what can and cannot legally be taken into account in the justification of a sentence. Why, it might be asked, should the judge not be concerned with the character of the criminal when she determines sentence? The question at issue, because a normative element in any distinction between law and morality is inevitable, is whether the normative element of the distinction offered is defensible. We should begin by trying to locate that element more precisely. It is not in the judge's concern with intention or motive. That concern may well have to do with the "mental element" of the crime, an element that is a necessary condition of the criminality of the act. It is not in judicial talk about prior offenses, dangerousness of the criminal to other persons, or the seriousness of the offense. All of this discussion can easily be shown to be relevant to the concern with the justice of the sentence, the public well-being, or retribution for what was done.

The normative element is, rather, this: The judge should not, in attempting to justify a sentence, argue that the criminal has a morally good or bad character. The clear case of such an argument is one that claims that the criminal has virtues or vices that are irrelevant to the nature of the crime he has committed, to his danger to society, or to the comparative justice of the sentence. For example, it might be argued that even though he has committed murder he is kind to his mother, pays his taxes on time, and is loyal to his friends. The reason that sort of consideration seems out of place in a court of law is that the judge does not ordinarily have standing to pass judgment on the character of the criminal.

To "pass judgment" in a morally indefensible way is to offer gratuitous judgment on a person's character. The judgment is gratuitous to the degree that the person judging has no good reason why she need judge. Members of a community do have such a need. They must decide what to think of a person because they must live with him. They must trust him or not, allow him responsibilities or not, beware of him or not. The judge's primary concern is with the case: She is, in sentencing, saying what is or is not to be tolerated, what justice demands. It is not her primary concern to say what kind of people are the "right sort." She is not appointed as an assayer of character but to see that justice is done under the law.

She is not ordinarily, in industrial countries, the representative of the particular community within which moral assessment of character is necessary, so much as an official of a system of law that makes the development and maintenance of such communities possible.

To whatever degree the judge does accept and is accepted in the role of character–assayer for the community, most typically in nonindustrial societies, she *is* justified in making appraisals of character. But, even so, she cannot take character assessment as her primary responsibility. She is not, except in purely paternalistic systems, appointed to maximize courage and honesty and to minimize cowardice and dishonesty but to do what she can about acts that are wrong under a legal code. The code does not prohibit cowardice or enjoin honesty but prohibits robbery and requires the payment of taxes.

It is difficult even to conceive of a code that prohibits some character traits and requires others. A part of the conceptual difficulty revolves around the nature of such traits. They are determinable rather than determinate. Honesty, for example, is not exhibited in just one way; it is exhibited in indefinitely many ways, depending on the context. It must therefore be inculcated in children over time and can almost never be said to be completely inculcated. The legal requirement with respect to character would then have to be that a certain standard of honesty be attained. But it is hard to see how that standard would be specified without reverting to a code that prohibits or requires acts. Otherwise, it is not clear how a point could be chosen at which the law would intervene in the development of character.

Even if such a code were possible, there would be good reason not to want it. This is so because ideals of moral perfection are many. In industrialized democratic societies, we live in a world of competing models of moral excellence. It is unclear how, except by fiat, a decision is to be made in favor of one model over another. To empower a legislature or a judge to make such decisions is to raise the unwelcome possibility of a world in which the most fundamental personal moral decision, that concerning the kind of person one should try to be, is abdicated to authority.

SOME COMPLICATIONS OF THIS VIEW

Whatever the merits of the proposed distinction between moral and legal concerns, it would not be wise to suppose that the distinction offered here, or any other distinction, can or should build an impermeable boundary between the two. Inevitably, there will be legal-like questions of moral rights, duties, and obligations; and just as inevitably, moral considerations will enter into the process of legislation, adjudication, and enforcement. It may be instructive to note one way in which this can occur: the moral evaluation of role players within a legal system.

The assumption of a role—of judge, lawyer, or warden, for example—both empowers and protects a person.[2] The grant of power is clear; the protection is from a kind of moral opprobrium that might otherwise apply. The "hanging judge" may be a member in good standing of church and country club. The general issue that is raised is whether and with what qualifications the role player is rightly, in virtue of his role, endowed with a kind of moral Teflon that deflects criticisms that might otherwise be relevant. One answer is that ordinary standards of judgment do not apply if the role in question is played under the rules of a morally defensible practice. Thus, for example, if the practice of punishment is justified, judges may do to other people what non–role players morally ought *not* to do. Another answer is to insist, as Leo Tolstoy does, that ordinary standards of morality apply right across the board and that no one ought to think herself entitled to do to another person as a judge or prosecutor what she could not morally do as a person who lacks the protection of those roles.

The entanglement of questions of individual character with those concerning the moral status of official acts or policies can be more intricate even than that. Even if the Teflon principle is allowed to apply to the official actions or decisions of a prosecutor or judge, he may suffer a closer than ordinary scrutiny of his private morality. One explanation of this may be that such role players must themselves be judges of more than legal propriety: they must be trusted to have a well-developed capacity for discriminating moral right from wrong. A morally disreputable personal life suggests the absence of that sort of capacity.[3]

CONCLUSION

In this chapter, we examined the suggestion that the primary concern of law is with behavior, with what or what not to do, and that the primary concern of morality is with character, with what kind of person to be. Whether or not this allocation of responsibilities between law and morality is acceptable, there will remain many areas of tension between morality and law. In the next two chapters, we will examine some of those tensions.

NOTES

1. We are speaking here of the criterion of what is to count as a virtue, not of the motive for being virtuous. We are not saying that the motive is that one wants to be preferred to other people.

2. As we noticed in Chapter 1, Tolstoy was vividly conscious of one moral issue that this fact about roles generates. His outrage, right or wrong, was triggered by the very existence of a system within which a set of role players could do to an individual what no one of the persons inhabiting a role would even think of doing were he not playing the role. No judge would

personally kill a defendant, for example. The practice of legal punishment, insofar as it creates roles within which people can avoid personal responsibility for what they do, is thus, for Tolstoy, morally repugnant.

3. For a perceptive analysis of the intricacies of the moral assessment of role players, see Nagel, Ch. 6.

CHAPTER 11

Moral Pressures on the Law

Laws may be criticized as unjust and may for that or other reasons be violated on grounds of conscience. In this chapter, we take up some of the resulting ways in which there can be "moral pressure" on the law.

INJUSTICE IN EGALITARIAN LEGAL SYSTEMS

Speaking of life in Europe after the fall of Rome, Prosper Boissonade tells us that, while Rome

> had fused within herself all classes and all races, and had brought them into an equality beneath her laws . . . [t]he Germanic customs established profound inequalities between the diverse peoples of the barbarian states. In Gaul there were as many as seven different codes of law, according to the origin of the inhabitants, Romans, Salian, Riparian, and Chamavian Franks, Burgundians, Visigoths, and Alamanni. High barriers separated the different social ranks, to each of which a different penal legislation was applied, shamefully indulgent towards the upper classes and barbarously harsh towards the lower, for whom were reserved the punishments of mutilation and torture. (p. 20)

We may take Boissonade's description of the government of fifth-century Gaul as a paradigm of unjust legal systems only if we are, as most of the readers of this book will be, egalitarians—egalitarians, that is, in that we believe that origin and class should not serve to differentiate us under the law. Were we not to believe this, but to think that the Chamavian Franks, say, deserved harsher punishment than did the Alamanni for the same crime because they were inferior to the Alamanni, then we might see no injustice in such a system.

We should note in passing that (however implausible this may be in fact) Germanic law *could* have been fairly administered *within* the different classes that it recognized. Chamavian Franks could have been given fair trials, findings of guilt or innocence could have been made with regard to due process of law, and sentences could have been carefully and impartially determined. There is, in short, no necessary inconsistency between justice in the application of law and injustice in the system of laws being applied. If a basic principle of justice is that relevantly like cases should be treated alike and relevantly different cases differently, then we need to know what is to count as relevant. If a legal system accepts considerations of origin or class as relevant, those considerations may weigh in the just determination of guilt or of a sentence under that unjust system.

It is of some importance to distinguish between injustice of a legal system and injustice in the application of its laws because failure to make such a distinction may lead to confusion about egalitarianism as an ideal. It is a necessary but not a sufficient condition of an egalitarian legal system that it be administered according to the principle we have mentioned. On that principle, only legally relevant matters will be considered in the disposition of cases before the bar. What then is a sufficient condition of an egalitarian system? That is a very difficult question. We have said already that an egalitarian system has a dually negative requirement. Neither my class nor my origin should have a bearing on my guilt under the law. It will not matter in an egalitarian system that my grandfather was a Jew, nor that I am a ditch digger. But this provision, as we can see at once, is complex. Surely there are some origins and classes that may well matter under a just legal system. It may matter, under affirmative action, that I am the descendant of a slave. Or it may be relevant, for tax purposes, that I am a member of the class of persons whose income is over $10,000 a year.

What is needed, although it is very difficult to provide, is a way of distinguishing acceptable from unacceptable legal distinctions of origin or class. (I will speak henceforth only of class because grouping people by their origins *is*, logically if not sociologically speaking, a way of relegating them to a particular class under the law.) Perhaps the best we can do for present purposes is to say that a distinction of class, within the law, is *un*acceptable—from the point of view of egalitarianism —if the distinction serves to disadvantage the persons falling in that class *merely* for the advantage of others who do not fall in that class. Thus, a rule that prohibits Blacks from using the public swimming pool serves merely to the supposed advantage of non-Blacks who want to go swimming. But a rule that prohibits carriers of a waterborne infectious disease from using the public pool is for the advantage of everyone, including the present disease carriers when they are not ill. A head tax on all Jews benefits other taxpayers by reducing overall taxes but carries no benefit at all for Jews. On the other hand, a real estate tax on the class of property holders is acceptable because, at least in principle, the revenue benefits everyone, including property holders.

If we were to refine this distinction, we should obviously have to say a good deal more about it. For example, we should have to mention that the classes of Jews, Blacks, and Chamavian Franks have this in common: One becomes a member by birth, and one is unalterably a member through the whole of one's life. There is no possibility that under some circumstances the legally disadvantaged Jew, Black, or Frank may stand, or may have stood, in a different relation to a law applicable to her by virtue of her class membership—may be or have been advantaged by the same law. Members of these classes differ, in this respect, from members of classes like that of property holders or tubercular persons. The former are permanently and irremediably disadvantaged by a law that singles them out for disadvantage on the basis of their "race." Thus, on a continuum of legal systems that aim for equality under the law, racially classified systems would be at or near the lower end.

THREE MORAL PRINCIPLES FOR THE CRITICISM OF LAW

The notion of a continuum suggests that there is not one but many ideals of egalitarianism. As we have seen, even at the lower end of such a continuum of legal systems, unjust laws may be justly administered. What counts as the highest end of such an egalitarian continuum is a very difficult question, as we can see when economic status is counted as a weight on the scale. Lowell, let us say, contends that the system is unjust because it accords him a salary equal to that of Robinson even though he, Lowell, works at a more highly skilled job. He is a glassblower, and Robinson sweeps the floor of the glassware plant. Coleridge, the manager of the plant, earns a salary that is twenty times greater than Robinson's salary. Robinson contends that such a distribution of the cost of production is unjust, that there should be no more difference than a multiple of five between the lowest and highest salaries.

It begins to be apparent that there is no sharp boundary between legal and economic systems. The minimum wage and the tax scale are set by law; in principle, if not in political reality, total incomes could be set by law, or citizens could be taxed according to their yearly expenditures. It is in principle possible that the ratio of earnings between labor and management could be set by law. Unless we confine the term *legal system* to the formal structure and mode of operation of legislatures, courts, and administrative agencies, economic considerations are likely to enter into our evaluation of a given system as more or less just.

Perhaps the best summary of this reflection on egalitarian justice under the law is that we must distinguish between the justice of a legal system and the degree to which the system operates for the benefit of everyone who falls under it. While these objectives of law cannot easily be disentangled, we may still think of them as separate standards against which a given system can be measured. We can summarize what we have said so far in the form of principles:

1. Relevantly like cases should be treated alike, and relevantly different cases treated differently.

2. No class of persons should be permanently and irremediably disadvantaged merely for the advantage of other classes of persons.

3. The system of law as a whole should be designed to operate for the advantage of everyone alike.

We now have, as egalitarians, a basis for the moral criticism of systems of law as more or less just. This not to say that these principles taken together provide a sufficient condition for the justice of a legal system. To provide such a condition, if it is possible at all, is far beyond the scope of this study (and the powers of the author). Each principle is, at best, a necessary condition of a just system.

The first two principles concern the fairness of the system; the last articulates the assumption necessary to justify the disadvantaging that is inevitable under a mutually beneficial system. John Rawls argues that even under a just system there will be role-related differences between the goods to which people are entitled. Rawls holds that any such differences ought to be to the advantage even of those who are worst off under the system adopted (Rawls, 152ff.). Whether justice requires that this condition be met is a subject of philosophical debate. Principle 3 is a less rigorous condition in that it does not demand that each law-gained advantage be justifiable as in the interest of the worst off. It does not require the Coleridges to show the Robinsons that they, the Robinsons, would be worse off if the Coleridges make less than they do. It only requires that the overall aim of the system of laws be to enhance the well-being of each of those who fall under it. Under the principle, Coleridge's advantages may be "free" in that the economic system produces them in its bounty, even though they can't be shown to be in Robinson's interest. Coleridge and Robinson may not be playing a "zero-sum game," one in which Coleridge's gain is Robinson's loss and vice versa. Claims and counterclaims of injustice and justice presuppose that there is such a game.

UTILITY AS A MORAL CRITERION OF LAW

That is a point that David Hume (1711–1776) makes vivid. Justice, Hume says, is "a cautious, jealous virtue." Were there no comparison of your rewards to mine, no looking over the shoulder at the other person's gains under the system, no envy, there would be no occasion for rules governing distribution of what is good and bad, of advantages and disadvantages under law. To illustrate this point, Hume imagines societies in which questions of justice simply would not arise. In one such society, every person is supplied with everything she could possibly desire, as perhaps on some tropical island where clothing, shelter, food, and entertainment are present in such abundance for everyone that there is no room for envy. Whatever is wanted is there for the taking. In another society, everyone is in such complete poverty that there simply is nothing to distribute between them, therefore no quarrels about who gets what. A third imagined society is composed of two classes, a superior and an inferior. The inferior class has absolutely no self-interest but only ardently desires to serve in every way possible the interest of the superior class. There is then never an occasion on which the inferiors would complain about the share of good things that goes to the superiors. Hume argues that in this latter society there would be no relations of justice between the inferior and superior societies (Sec. III).

The moral of Hume's speculative remarks is not that justice is an inferior or despicable virtue of practices and institutions. Hume's imaginary societies are counterfactual, and that is the point. We do not live in any such societies. Given that we do not and that there is concern with getting one's share, it behooves us to invent practices that apportion shares to the Robinsons, Lowells, and Coleridges according to principles that can be accepted by them in advance as fair. That is the insight of contract theories of justice from Thomas Hobbes to John Rawls. For such theorists, the chief task is the delineation of such principles.

The chief opposition to the contract theorist's approach is, as the reader may suspect, that of the utilitarians or, in the broadest rendering of that position, of the consequentialists. The latter are theorists, remember, who hold that there is one supreme principle in morality: It is only the best possible balance of good consequences over bad that can make one practice preferable to another. What counts as good consequences is a matter for debate—classic utilitarians like Jeremy Bentham and John Stuart Mill holding that it is the happiness of everyone concerned. Modern utilitarians tend to interpret happiness as satisfaction: Those are happiest whose desires are most fully satisfied.

What becomes of egalitarian justice on such a theory? Principle 1—like cases should be treated alike and different cases differently—is mandatory simply because there is more total satisfaction under a system that is in this way predictable and orderly. Utilitarians agree with Principle 3—the system of law as a whole should be designed to operate for the advantage of everyone, where advantage is understood to mean the maximization of satisfaction over the community. But they may bog down on the phrase "everyone alike" because that implies that no minority's satisfaction may be sacrificed for the overall increase of satisfaction. Where the utilitarian theory comes most violently into collision with contract theorists is over Principle 2—no class should be irremediably disadvantaged for the advantage of other classes. It is difficult, if not impossible, for a utilitarian to accept this principle because the overall happiness might be increased by the abject servitude of a few. The best that the utilitarian can do is to argue that overall happiness is unlikely to be enhanced by any such system.

The principles by which we can measure the justice of a legal system are thus at best partially reconcilable with utilitarianism. In truth, that theory is unlikely ever to satisfy the advocates of those principles just because it claims hegemony for the utilitarian principle. *Any* selection of the principles of justice can be at best, on the utilitarian theory, secondary principles. That is, they can only be principles that, if generally followed, will likely result in greater overall happiness — currently understood as satisfaction. The difficulty is that it is impossible on utilitarian premises to rule out occasions on which it might pay in increased general satisfaction to underplay or ignore Principles 1 or 2. It might best accord with the calculation of satisfactions to leave some one class of persons, however small, in misery.

If the utilitarian argues that that eventuality is extremely unlikely, given the utilitarian advantage of predictability and regularity under a system of law, still the advocate of the principles is unlikely to be pacified. He will say that what is advocated is a principle, not a bargaining counter. To advocate a principle is to say, so he will argue, that there is a limit beyond which law should not go in the interest of expediency. It is to say that to entrust the protection of minorities to the outcome of a calculation of satisfaction is at best to hope that the principles of justice will not be violated. But that is not the same as making a principled stand, drawing a boundary over which one will not step.

A FOURTH PRINCIPLE

So far, we have been concerned with the *egalitarian* justice or injustice of a system of law. However, there may be nonegalitarian considerations that point to the injustice of a legal system. Why might it be argued, for example, that a legal system that allows no excuses, a strict liability system, is unjust? Let us try to imagine a system of legal prohibitions and requirements in which no room at all is left for such defenses as insanity, accident, mistake, or in fact any of the defenses we discussed in Chapter 6. Keats, picking rare poppies on the rim of the Grand Canyon, is shoved in anger by Shelley (an amateur ecologist whose short fuse is ignited by what she sees as the wanton destruction of an endangered species). The shove bowls Keats into Byron, who staggers over the edge to his death. A jury finds that it was Keats's impact on Byron that was the proximate cause of Byron's death. Keats is charged with . . . what? How are we to distinguish degrees of homicide in the absence of excuses? We are reduced to one degree, so the charge is simply homicide, the punishment for which is, say, ten years in prison. Shelley, whose anger has increased exponentially in the interim, now hunts down and machine-guns a second poppy picker. She, too, is charged; and both Keats and Shelley are convicted and sentenced to ten years in prison.

I will assume that a legal system that treats wrongdoers in this way treats them inequitably, that it is an unjust system. But why is it unjust? It is not easy, if possible at all, to account for its injustice in terms of the three principles that we have recognized so far in this chapter. We want to say that Keats's and Shelley's cases should not be treated alike because they are not relevantly alike. But why not? The law says that he who commits homicide goes to the penitentiary for ten years. Both committed homicide. Does the law violate the second principle? Does it permanently and irremediably disadvantage the one class for the advantage of another? But what are the "classes" here? How does Keats's having an excuse, morally speaking, make him a member of a class in the appropriate sense in which, as a member of a class, he can be permanently disadvantaged? The next time he is a wrongdoer under the law, he may have no excuse. Then, if the talk of advantage and disadvantage makes sense here at all, he will be a member of the advantaged class. That is, he will now, like Shelley, only have to suffer under the law what persons who had an excuse suffer. We would have to stretch the notions of class and advantage unmercifully to account for the injustice of a pure and full strict liability system. "Pure," in that no excuses are ever allowed; "full" in that (unlike the Universal No-Fault Insurance scheme discussed in Chapter 6, which concerns only the allocation of losses) it extends to all legal prohibitions and requirements.

Principle 3—the legal system should be for the benefit of everyone alike—is at best ambiguously relevant to the injustice of such a system. Someone like Barbara Wootton might argue for the overall advantage of such a system. But how are we to say what "alike" means if we can draw no distinction between Keats's and Shelley's violations of the law, excuses being ruled out in advance as relevant?

In short, the kind of pressure morality exerts on the law here, a pressure that inhibits the spread of strict liability law, is not so much concerned with egalitarian justice as with justice of another kind. The appropriate standard of justice here, a non- (but not anti-) egalitarian one, might be expressed in some such principle as this:

4. Legal penalties and punishments should fall only on those who are responsible for violations of the law.

In Chapter 7, we offered an argument for the practice of responsibility–ascription, at least in those areas of law in which losses must somehow be allocated across a population. Whether that argument is conclusive and whether it can be extended beyond civil to criminal law, there is at least an apparent injustice in a system that takes no account of excuses or, more generally, of defenses against a charge of wrongdoing.

CONSCIENTIOUS VIOLATION OF THE LAW

So far, we have spoken of moral pressures on the law in a theoretical way. That is, we have considered principles of justice that seem to draw boundaries for legal systems. "Pressure" may here seem a rather ethereal matter. But we should also notice a much more direct and earthy kind of moral pressure against legal systems: violation of law on grounds of conscience. From the Boston Tea Party to current taxpayers' revolts, from refusals to return slaves to their legal owners to Vietnam-era draft card burners, American history is full of examples of such violations.

Some cautions should be noted in discussion of moral pressure on particular laws. Not all conscientious violation of the law is meant to constitute pressure to change the law violated, or indeed any particular law at all. Those who lie down in front of trucks loaded with nerve-gas cylinders are not protesting the law prohibiting obstruction of a public roadway; and divers who plug the outlets of polluting industrial plants may have nothing against the laws of trespass. Also, not every legal rule demands obedience. Particular rules may come in conflict with more abstract legal rules or principles; the decision whether to continue in a rule-governed role may be an open one; or there may be generally acceptable breaches of a rule.[1] We are concerned here only with protests and refusals that are aimed at changing a law (not necessarily by violating *that* law) and with pressures against laws that do in fact demand obedience.

Defenders of a given legal system may want very much to find ways, within the system, to accommodate conscientious violation of law. They may rightly believe this necessary if the system is to survive; and they may, also rightly, regard a system that contains avenues and byways for conscientious objectors as morally more defensible than one that does not. It would require an extraordinary degree of optimistic obtuseness to suppose that a legal system contains and will contain *no* laws that morally deserve to be ignored or consciously violated.

If this be granted, then what modes of response to conscientious violation are open to prosecutors, judges, and other officials of a legal system? One method is simply not to enforce the law in question by failure to arrest, prosecute, or bring to trial. Two dangers should be recognized in this method. One is that what we have listed as our first principle of justice may be violated: Like cases may not be treated alike. Robinson conscientiously violates a law for which nonconscientious violator Frost is tried and convicted. How can we justify to Frost the nonprosecution of Robinson? What seems to be required, and may be difficult but not impossible to provide, is a more fine-tuned criterion or set of criteria than is provided by the blunt distinction between conscientious and nonconscientious violation. The blunt distinction may be all that is necessary when the law violated is itself morally questionable, such as the law that slaves must be returned to owners. But more commonly, the laws violated—laws of trespass or public nuisance, say—are broken in the interest of protesting a government policy like benign neglect of environmental decay or undeclared war with another nation.

The second danger in selective nonenforcement of law is that this is a practice that, if generalized, leaves great and difficult-to-control power in the hands of police, prosecutors, and judges. There is thus the danger not only of unequal treatment but also of the unbridled abuse of power for the purposes of those who wield it. Given large and ill-defined groups of offenders who are not to be prosecuted, it may become progressively less clear who ought to be prosecuted. This is a situation made to order for vengeful, resentful, envious, or angry officials to have their way with offenders. That this is a danger more to nonconscientious than to conscientious offenders renders it no less dangerous to public well-being. Here again, the only remedy is to clarify as much as possible the standard that must be met for nonprosecution of those whose violations are conscientious. The remaining problem, raised by the very process of clarification, is the justified uneasiness with a process by which what is the law is, at least semiofficially, declared not to apply, practically speaking, to a whole class of persons to whom under law it does in fact apply.

Similar but not insurmountable difficulties attend the second means of accommodating the legal system to conscientious violators. This is the option of treating such offenders more leniently than nonconscientious lawbreakers. This option can be pursued not only at the level of sentencing but also by prosecution for a lesser offense, early parole, parole under easier than ordinary conditions, amelioration of the punishment otherwise due, or even legislative or executive pardon of conscientious offenders. The same problems about equality under the law and the possible abuse of authority arise, and the same issue becomes central: how and in what way to lay down criteria by which conscientious violation can be distinguished from ordinary criminal behavior (Greenawalt, pp. 276–277).

It is unreasonable to think that those criteria can be merely formal ones designed to show that it is really for *conscientious* reasons that the law was broken. That Price's conscience directs her to rid the world of the president of the United States entitles her to no special consideration by officials of the legal system. It is equally unreasonable to lay down the requirement that the reasons for violation be universally accepted. It does not diminish Wells's status as a conscientious offender if his belief that the Vietnam War should be resisted is not universally shared. The trick is to find criteria relevant to distinguishing those who are entitled to special treatment on grounds of conscience from ordinary offenders. If the criteria cannot be merely formal ones, they will inevitably involve normative judgment of what does and does not count as a good moral reason for violation of the law. If those reasons become widely accepted, the law will likely fade away through lack of enforcement, repeal, or judicial evisceration.

WHAT IS A GOOD REASON FOR CONSCIENTIOUS VIOLATION?

What then *is* a good moral reason? Why should not your good reason be, or my not-so-good or even bad reason, for violation of law? How can government policy concerning conscientious violation rest on such shifting ground? Do we not need a theoretical criterion that will determine what is and is not a good moral reason? Consequentialism attempts to provide such a criterion, as does contract theory. But to move toward a version of one of these theories may be to move too fast.

The theories are inconsistent with one another, and there are differing and inconsistent versions of each theory. Attempts to reconcile these inconsistencies have been less than successful. It would be better to begin further back, to ask whether the metaphor of shifting ground may not be misleading. *Are* there significant differences over what counts as a moral reason? *Do* inconsistencies in reasons for conscientious violation necessarily imply inconsistent government policy toward the conscientious lawbreaker?

There is one sort of reason of conscience, mentioned earlier, of which legal reformers at least since Bentham have been rightly suspicious. Bentham argued that there is a class of reasons that falls under what he called, in irony, the Principle of Sympathy and Antipathy. As examples of appeals to this "principle," he mentions, among others, appeals to natural law, the will of God, right reason, common sense, and the moral sense. Bentham held that such argumentative moves have this in common: They refer to an "internal standard." That is, there is no public, impartial way of determining what the standards require. We are confidently told by Tweedledum that God, natural law, and common sense all require us to close down abortion clinics; Tweedledee appeals to the same authorities to support the right of women to abortion. If Tweedledum or Tweedledee violates the law in support of her belief, it is far from clear how such opposed readings of the same standard can be accepted as morally compelling (Bentham, Ch. IV).

Bentham contends that conduciveness to the happiness of everyone affected by a law or policy *is* a public standard. Calculations of the likely degree of happiness created (or destroyed) by a policy can turn out right or wrong. We can learn from experience and can thus make better or worse justified predictions by means of what Bentham called the "felicific calculus." But in Part One, in our discussion of punishment, we glimpsed some of the difficulties in the utilitarian position, enough to suggest that it may not provide the promised standard of moral right and wrong. Although we can share Bentham's suspicion of "internal standards" and can see the advantage of an external one, we may not yet be ready to embrace public happiness as *the* standard of morality.

Yet it would be moving much too fast to say that we are all at odds about what does and does not count as a weighty moral reason. Even if it is not easy to define happiness, still it would be hard to deny that we ought to take into account the effect of actions or policies on the happiness (or misery) of the people who would be affected by them. Given that there are different senses of egalitarian justice, some such principles as those we listed previously can surely capture much of what is meant by complaints of injustice.

But perhaps the chief caution that emerges from a search after a compelling distinction between good and bad moral reasons is that a government should attempt such a distinction only where it seems absolutely necessary. If the suggestion in Chapter 10 has merit, then law will be fundamentally concerned with what people may and may not *do*. Whatever reasons of conscience Tweedledee or Tweedledum may have, government must, in the interest of public order, restrain bombings, assaults, and trespass.

CONCLUSION

We listed four commonly accepted principles for the moral criticism of systems of law in a society in which egalitarian ideals are a given. We then discussed the kinds of criticism implicit in refusal to obey a law on grounds of conscience. Here we noticed a few of the complications involved in the morally desirable attempt of a legal system to accommodate itself to well-founded moral violations of law. We turn now to "legal pressures on morality," specifically to attempts to "enforce morality" or to mandate a program of moral education.

NOTES

1. These points are expanded in Greenawalt, Sect. I.

Legal Pressures on Morality

If the law's proper concern is with behavior, then governing bodies must decide what acts to prohibit, permit, or require. But how can a government do that without appeal, tacit or explicit, to some moral standard? Is it not at least a part of the law's business to enforce morality? In this chapter, we examine arguments both for and against the legal enforcement of morality. We also have a look at a related problem, that of government-mandated programs of moral education.

MALA IN SE

What we need first is a clear example of a law that is intended to enforce morality. Many laws seem to have little or nothing to do with the requirements of morality. We are prohibited by law from driving without a license, from posting signs along an interregional highway, or from broadcasting on an unassigned frequency. These are examples of what have sometimes been called *mala prohibita*. The wrongdoing is, so to speak, the child of the law. Before the enactment of the law, there was no such wrongdoing. It is customary to contrast such laws with *mala in se*, laws that prohibit what is "in itself" wrong.[1]

We need, then, a *malum in se* prohibited by law *on the ground that* it is immoral. Examples come easily to mind that will not do for our purpose. Assault, rape, and murder are morally wrong and are at the same time legally prohibited. But the legal prohibition is persuasively explicable on grounds other than the enforcement of morality. If a government would preserve order and make civilized life possible, it must prohibit activities of this kind. The justification for criminalizing them need have nothing to do with the protection, enforcement, or reinforcement of morality. Morality need not be mentioned or thought of in defending the right of government to arrest, try, and imprison people for murder, rape, and assault. It is enough to say that life is too dangerous and civilized life impossible in the absence of such government power. We need then an example of a law that is enacted and enforced for the reason that what it prohibits is immoral. That is, the act or activity need not be dangerous or prejudicial to civilized common life. Its perpetrators must be imprisoned or otherwise punished just because what they have done is morally wrong or abhorrent. What sort of act would that be?

"THE LAW'S BUSINESS": HOMOSEXUAL BEHAVIOR

An example frequently cited in the heated debates on this subject is of sexual acts done in private between consenting adults. In a famous debate, Lord Patrick Devlin, a British jurist, takes issue with the "Report of the Committee on Homosexual Offences and Prostitution." That report, commonly known as the "Wolfenden Report," rejects the criminalization of homosexual acts done in private between consenting adults. The criminal law's function, according to the committee,

> is to preserve public order and decency, to protect the citizen from what is offensive or injurious, and to provide sufficient safeguards against exploitation and corruption of others, particularly those who are specially vulnerable because they are young, weak in body or mind, inexperienced, or in a state of special physical, official or economic dependence.
>
> It is not, in our view, the function of the law to intervene in the private lives of citizens, or to seek to enforce any particular pattern of behavior, further than is necessary to carry out the purposes we have outlined.
>
> . . . Unless a deliberate attempt is to be made by society, acting through the agency of the law, to equate the sphere of crime with that of sin, there must remain a realm of private morality and immorality which is, in brief and crude terms, not the law's business. To say this is not to condone or encourage private immorality. (Quoted in Devlin, pp. 2–3)

Devlin rejects this conception of the "law's business" as overly restrictive. Society, he says, "may use the law to preserve morality in the same way it uses it to safeguard anything else that is essential to its existence" (p. 11). It is essential to a society's existence that it be protected from dangers originating outside of the society. This is what justifies the enactment and enforcement of laws against treason. Why not then protect society from dangers that originate from within?

> . . . [A]n established morality is as necessary as good govern-
> ment to the welfare of society. Societies disintegrate from
> within more frequently than they are broken up by external
> pressures. There is disintegration when no common morality
> is observed. . . . [S]ociety is justified in taking the same steps
> to preserve its moral code as it does to preserve its govern-
> ment and other essential institutions. . . . The suppression of
> vice is as much the law's business as the suppression of sub-
> versive activities. (Devlin, pp. 13–14)

Self-preservation is so fundamental an objective of government, Devlin maintains, that it warrants whatever legislation may be necessary to achieve it. Thus,
any attempt to set off a realm of privacy within which the law may not intrude
must, where self-preservation is at issue, be set aside. What people do in the
privacy of their homes may threaten the continued existence of the state quite as
much as what they do in public. We must balance the protection of privacy against
the protection of society:

> You may argue that if a man's sins affect only himself it can-
> not be the concern of society. If he chooses to get drunk
> every night in the privacy of his own home, is any one except
> himself the worse for it? But suppose a quarter or a half of the
> population got drunk every night, what sort of society
> would it be? . . . The same may be said of gambling. (Devlin,
> p. 14)

THE REASONABLE MAN

How are we to decide then that an activity is so immoral as to threaten to break
down the moral code and thus endanger the continued existence of society? What,
first, for the purposes of the law, will be the criterion of immorality? Surely there
are many people, even if a minority, who would today argue that homosexuality
is *not* immoral. Devlin would have us repair here to our old legal friend, the
reasonable man:

> If the reasonable man believes that a practice is immoral and
> believes also — no matter whether the belief is right or wrong,
> so be it that it is honest and dispassionate — that no right-
> minded member of his society could think otherwise, then
> for the purpose of the law it is immoral. (p. 23)

The test then is not majority opinion. But what, more exactly, is it? The
reasonable man cannot be the person who merely has reasons for his moral belief.

Surely most homosexuals could give reasons for their beliefs. It cannot be even the person who has better reasons than those with whom he disagrees. That would be to make the test whether the belief is true; but Devlin explicitly rules out any such test and understandably so. There is no moral tribunal that will determine authoritatively which of our moral beliefs are true; in the absence of such a tribunal, the test would be useless. What we seem to need then, if we are to make use of the reasonable man test, is a noncircular criterion by means of which we can distinguish reasonable from nonreasonable persons. We cannot allow the advocate of the criminalization of homosexuality, as an immoral practice, to accept as reasonable only those persons who agree that it is immoral. But how to specify a noncircular criterion?

That this is a difficulty for Devlin is apparent. Still, he might answer that the reasonable man standard is one that works well enough in other areas of law, even in the absence of any clear criterion by means of which we can distinguish reasonable from unreasonable or unreasoning men. It works not as a formal but as a practical standard. Judges and juries may apply that standard simply as a way of distancing themselves from their own prejudices and biases. At the least, it prohibits direct appeal to Jeremy Bentham's Principle of Sympathy and Antipathy. We should note that Devlin's argument may seem weakened in a time in which there is increasing tolerance of homosexuality. But, despite Devlin's personal dislike of homosexual practices, he might, were there a consensus of reflective persons that such practices are acceptable, have to concede that the reasonable man would not regard them as so wrong as to require the law for their suppression.

The fact is that Devlin's argument, more closely examined, does not attempt to show that immorality should be punished simply because that it what it is. His proposal is rather doubly hypothetical. If a practice threatens to break down a moral consensus *and* if the consensus is a necessary condition of the survival of a society, then the society ought to prohibit the practice and to punish those who engage in it. The argument thus rests upon empirical claims, albeit claims of a high order of abstraction. Does a given practice threaten to undermine the consensus of which the reasonable man is the supposed embodiment? And does the continued existence of the society indeed rest on the consensus in question? Would the society "break down" were the consensus to be violated? Devlin does not provide evidence that failure to punish homosexual practices between consenting adults in private would have such dire consequences.

DEVLIN'S "MORALITY"

Devlin's argument then is also consequential and one that admits, despite its absolutist tone, a certain moral relativism. When he speaks of "morality," he means what representative people in a given social order at a given time and place firmly believe to be right or wrong. And he is not, in the last analysis, saying that it is because it is wrong that the practice should be punished but that it should be punished to preserve that social order. But is every social order morally entitled to preservation? Are there not social orders like Caligula's Rome or Hitler's Germany that morally deserve dissolution? What we seem to need if we are to find an answer to that question is a distinction between differing conceptions of "social order." On one understanding, the assumed successor of social order and the danger faced in its dissolution is anarchy, a condition in which, according to Thomas Hobbes (1588–1679), there is a war of all against all and

> there is no place for industry; because the fruit thereof is uncertain: and consequently no culture of the earth; no navigation, no use of commodities that may be imported by sea; no commodious building . . . no arts; no letters; no society; and which is worst of all, continual fear and danger of violent death; and the life of man, solitary, poor, nasty, brutish, and short. (Ch. 13)

Supposing that this were the alternative to Hitler's Germany, the argument that the consensus holding society together should not be undermined is worthy of notice. The price of dissolution would be a heavy one. But the dissolution of a given social order, although it might entail a period of lawlessness, nearly invariably gives rise to another social order. Even if it were reluctantly granted that a Hitler's or Caligula's social order is preferable to anarchy, it does not follow that those orders are preferable to any order whatever that might succeed them. To hold that they were would amount to a morally indefensible endorsement of a ghastly status quo.

What is the "morality" that is to be enforced by appropriate legislation? We have been satisfied so far to consider the example of homosexual activity in private between consenting adults. But what is the more general conception of morality that informs Devlin's argument that morality should be enforced? Devlin holds that by threat of imprisonment or other punishment persons should be made fearful enough not to do what otherwise they would do. As H. L. A. Hart points out, this proposed policy implies an impoverished notion of what it is to be moral:

> . . . [W]here there is no harm to be prevented and no potential victim to be protected, as is often the case where conventional sexual morality is disregarded, it is difficult to understand the assertion that conformity, even if motivated merely by fear of the law's punishment is a value worth pursuing, notwithstanding the misery and sacrifice of freedom that it involves. The attribution of value to mere conforming behavior, in abstraction from both motive and consequences, belongs not to morality but to taboo. . . . [W]hat is valuable . . . is *voluntary* restraint, not submission to coercion, which seems quite empty of moral value. (1966, Ch. III)

Devlin might grant that a society in which there is mere conformity to an externally imposed and enforced set of rules need not be a moral one. He might hold that if there is to be the kind of consensus that holds a society together people must, for the most part, act voluntarily as the moral code requires. But he might contend without inconsistency that nevertheless violations of the code should be punishable under the law. The difficulty with any such position, however, is that then motivation becomes blurred, even in the mind of the person who behaves as morally he should. Is he avoiding homosexual practices because he believes it to be wrong or because if he is caught he will go to jail?

The point might be more clear if we were to consider another less immediately controversial example. It is morally wrong to be ungrateful for favors given. A morally good man or woman will not be an ingrate. Suppose that ungratefulness were prohibited by law on pain of imprisonment. A special jail, like a nineteenth-century debtors' prison, is set aside for ingrates. A new subspecialty of Ingrate Law crops up within the practice of criminal law. District attorneys make their name by prosecution of spectacular cases of ungratefulness; political careers are ruined by indictment and conviction. How, as enforcement becomes more rigorous, are we then to distinguish between being genuinely grateful for favors done and doing what a grateful person might be expected to do so that one will not go to jail or be politically handicapped? As the actions or failures to act that are characteristic of ungratefulness diminish, do we then have a more grateful society?

"An enforced morality," then, may be an oxymoron. Earlier, we suggested that law is primarily concerned with behavior, with what or what not to do, and that morality is primarily concerned with what kind of person to be. It follows from that distinction, if it is accepted, that you cannot enforce gratefulness, kindness, courage, or loyalty—even if you can legally require acts that may be characteristic of those virtues.

Still, does not this apportionment of territory between law and morality suggest another, indirect way in which the law might enforce morality? Why can a government not legally mandate moral education that will help shape young people into the bearers of moral virtues? What, if anything, is wrong with legally required public moral education?

THREE POSSIBLE AIMS
OF LEGALLY REQUIRED MORAL EDUCATION

An analysis of any such proposal must begin with distinctions between different conceptions of moral education. What would be the aim of a moral-education curriculum?

1. To fashion children who will do what is right and avoid what is wrong

2. To instill the proper moral beliefs in children, to indoctrinate them

3. To encourage the development of moral traits of character, the virtues, and discourage the development of vices

While these global aims are overlapping, it will be worthwhile to say a few words in the attempt to distinguish them more clearly if we are to specify with even minimal precision what a legally mandated moral-education program might be like. The underlying issue is whether there is any conception of moral education or of enforcement such that we may meaningfully and truly say that enforced moral education is a desirable practice.

The difficulty with the first aim, that we produce children who will do what is right and not do what is wrong, is that this is consistent with a purely external, nonreflective conception of what it is to be moral. Suppose, assuming (counterfactually) that there is universal moral consensus on right and wrong and ignoring practical difficulties, we were to find a way to ensure that children *will* do what is right and not do what is wrong. Suppose that educational psychologists have devised a scheme of appropriate disciplines and reinforcements that, when properly administered, yields 100 percent success. No child who has endured the prescribed regimen will thereafter ever do wrong or fail to do right. This is to think of children as well-trained creatures, predictable indeed, but not necessarily moral because we do not know anything about the motives that impel them to behave as moral beings would. We can suspect that because their behavior is so very consistent, it must be by now a matter of artificially implanted instinct—as opposed to naturally instinctive behavior. It is behavior that does not require decision, determination, courage, or, above all, reasoning. To suppose that such a pattern of external behavior can serve as a sufficient condition of the morality of the beings that exhibit it is, to say the least, difficult.

The second aim, to indoctrinate children with proper moral beliefs, presents related difficulties. If to indoctrinate is to condition the child not to worry or reflect when faced with a moral choice but to act confidently on an unquestioned belief, then we may wonder whether that child has been morally educated. The general point about this and the first aim is that the development of critical intelligence is a necessary condition of achieving status as a moral person. Neither the first nor the second aim, properly qualified, can be considered irrelevant to moral education. A moral person *will* have certain instinctive reactions to the plight of others, well-developed repugnances for some kinds of behavior, and instincts of openness, generosity, and so on. He will *also* have some well-ingrained beliefs—for example, that deceptiveness and brutality are wrong. But it cannot be a sufficient condition of his counting as moral that he is a being who automatically and uncritically does and believes what moral beings do and believe.

The third possible aim of a moral-education program may be closer to the mark, the aim of developing certain personality traits, moral virtues, and avoiding the growth of others, moral vices. There will, on this understanding of moral education, be room for critical intelligence as well as the right instincts and beliefs. A government might require the schools to engage in moral education so understood. If it did so, however, the enforcement of morals would be at two important removes from that envisioned by Devlin. It would not criminalize behavior on the ground that it is immoral but would at most criminalize failure to provide or submit to moral education. And moral education itself would not consist in the mere control of behavior but would have an aim considerably more complex than that one.

THE DEMANDS OF LIBERTY

The complexity is generated in large part by the competing ideals of social well-being and individual liberty. John Stuart Mill (1806–1873) sets out the argument for allowing each individual the largest possible space for the development of her own character:

> As it is useful that while mankind is imperfect there should be different opinions, so it is that there should be different experiments of living; that free scope should be given to varieties of character, short of injury to others; and that the worth of different modes of life should be proved practically, when anyone thinks fit to try them. It is desirable, in short, that in things which do not primarily concern others individuality should assert itself. . . . Where not the person's own character but the traditions or customs of other people are the rule of conduct, there is wanting one of the principal ingredients of human happiness, and quite the chief ingredient of individual and social progress. (Ch. III)

But, as Mill notes, the boundaries of this liberty to engage in experiments in living are drawn by the principle that no one may engage in conduct that is prejudicial to the interests of others; and if public opinion and persuasion will not prevent such conduct, then the threat of punishment under the law is warranted.

We should note that Devlin in one way agrees with Mill. Devlin's argument is not "paternalistic," as that term is usually understood. It is not that the law should interfere in the private lives of citizens for their own good, the good of those particular citizens. It is out of concern for the well-being of society that he argues for the enforcement of morals. Nevertheless, he holds, against Mill, that behavior in private between consenting adults may erode social well-being and that it is not so easy as Mill supposes to isolate the social effects of private behavior. The difficulty with Devlin's argument is that if we are willing to count as socially dangerous any behavior done in private that would be repugnant to the elusive "reasonable man," then there is little or no space allowed for those experiments in living and self-formation of character that Mill considers so necessary to a rich and satisfying individual and common life.

As Mill is vividly aware, people may make use of their liberty to engage in experiments that are very much against their own long-term interest and that they will live to regret. He approves counseling, advice, and education to help developing beings avoid such choices. But when those beings arrive at normal adulthood, he would place the burden of proof on a government that attempts to control, by threat of punishment, how they live their lives in private.[2]

EDUCATION FOR CHARACTER

Although Mill offers us a provocative sketch of the relation between moral education and government force in the fostering of morality, the question of the content of moral education is still very much before us. We are concerned here with the form and content of *government-mandated* moral education. We will take it for granted, in the spirit of Mill's argument, that government has no business attempting to control all moral education. But if the relevant role of government is to discourage behavior that is against the common interest or that is injurious to the private interest of others and if that role can be played educationally rather than punitively, then what kind of education should government prescribe? One way to approach this question is to think of moral education as an indefinitely expansible project. To speak in the most general terms, the object is to encourage the development of the right sort of person.

While a few basic laws of the criminal code may, if properly enforced, relieve us of fears of Hobbesian anarchy, more is needed for a humane common life. We must not only abstain from murder, rape, and assault but also must develop some interest in and concern for others, some sense of what is and is not just, some sympathy for and tolerance of those who are not as strong or smart as we are, some sense that others have a right to live their lives in peace and with some expectation of help when it is sorely needed. The right sort of person will have developed these sympathies and understandings.[3]

One need not be a Devlinian to sense the crucial importance to society of the development of these qualities of character. Or should we not say, less sweepingly, to *our* society, our particular form of Western culture? What unifies the virtues, which we discussed as necessary to civilized life is that they moderate or constrain tendencies in our society that stem from very deep assumptions about and attitudes toward individual and common life. While there are countering tendencies and alternative modes, our lives, in the West in the twentieth century, tend to be competitive and egoistic. We are taught that the aim is to get ahead of the other person, that winning is what counts, that success is the goal of life. The virtues that best express this ethos are instrumental, qualities necessary if we are to succeed in the competition that shapes our understanding of the world in which we live. For example, we are taught to be persistent, cautious, hard-working, resourceful, and prompt to take advantage of whatever opportunity offers.

Yet we also recognize that a society composed of people with these and cognate qualities need not be desirable. Individuals concerned to pursue their own good or the good of those close to them may successfully do so while being brutal and uncaring in their relationships with others, if those others are perceived simply as competitors in a devil-take-the-hindmost competition. At least three enlargements of perspective are needed. The competition must be understood as fair; there must be respect for other persons as individuals, not merely as competitors; and there must be fellow-feeling for the wide range of human beings with whom one shares one's world. We might refer to these requirements, respectively, as the Principles of Fairness, Respect, and Sympathy—with the proviso that "principle" be understood very broadly. In the sense intended, a person not only accepts a principle as a supremely important reason but also the principle characterizes him: his motives, attitudes, expressions, and reactions. For a person to accept a principle is for him to be or try to be an exemplar of the Principles of Fairness, Respect, and Sympathy.

At the same time, it should be recognized that the attainment of these qualities of character, of these virtues, is an open-ended, never-ending task. Government-mandated moral education must be concerned with a more modest aim, the development of these virtues to the degree that public order, peace, and harmony demand. And these objectives must be understood as practicable minima. Too high a price in individual liberty might otherwise be paid in the interest of political comity.

CONCLUSION

The argument of this chapter has been that some legal pressure on morality is justified by the need to avoid anarchy and achieve minimal civility and harmony. This pressure can take two related forms: the enunciation and enforcement of prohibitions and requirements and a mandated minimal moral education. The focus of the chapter was initially on the enforcement of codes of conduct that are not obviously or are only debatably necessary for a civil society: as an example, laws restricting homosexual practices in private between consenting adults. No rationale for such legislation was found that would warrant the price in loss of individual liberty. This conclusion is, of course, quite consistent with criminalization of public or private conduct that harms other persons against their will (or presumed will). A required moral-education program, essential as it may be for common life, must nevertheless be carefully circumscribed in the interest of liberty. The price of a legally mandated detailed or extensive moral-education program would be a higher one than most citizens of a free democratic order would be willing to pay.

If, to take up the metaphor of Chapter 1, philosophy of law is a rambling ancient house with new additions and annexes, we have here explored only a very little of the whole structure. In rooms that we have not entered, we would have found, among other things, vigorous debates over the nature of justice, the aims and methods of legal reasoning, the underlying power structure of legal systems, and the nature of equality, liberty, and rights. We might also have discovered workshops and studies in which the philosophical implications of more ground-level practices like plea bargaining and preferential treatment were examined.

I hope that this book will have provided the reader with a useful and not-too-difficult-to-follow path into the larger subject of the philosophy of law.

NOTES

1. There are problems with such a distinction. To clarify it, we would need to know whether a *malum prohibitum* is such because it was logically impossible to do the wrong before the law's enactment or because before enactment the "wrong" act would have been morally indifferent or even right. Is it, for example, that before there were licenses, there could have been no such offense as driving without a license, or is it more like this: Posting signs on an interregional highway became an offense only with the enactment of a law prohibiting it? Or can *mala prohibita* be of either type?

2. For discussion of the political issues of moral education in a liberal demo-cratic state, see Gutmann, passim.

3. Needless to say, this is not the sort of person that has always and every-where been approved.

> The religion of these primitive ages was exclusively domestic; as also were morals. Religion did not say to a man, showing him another man, That is thy brother. It said to him, That is a stranger; he cannot participate in the religious acts of thy hearth; he cannot approach the tomb of thy family; he has other gods than thine, and cannot unite with thee in a com-mon prayer; thy gods reject his adoration, and regard him as thy enemy; he is thy foe also.
>
> In this religion of the hearth man never supplicates the divinity in favor of other men; he invokes him only for him-self and his. (Fustel de Coulanges, Ch. IX)

References

Abbott, Jack. 1981. *In the Belly of the Beast*. New York: Vintage Books.

Aquinas, St. Thomas. 1945 (1265–1273). *Summa Theologica*. In *Basic Writings of St. Thomas Aquinas*, A. C. Pegis, ed., Vol. II. New York: Random House.

Austin, John. 1954 (1832). *The Province of Jurisprudence Determined*. London: Weidenfeld and Nicolson.

Bentham, Jeremy. 1948 (1789). *An Introduction to the Principles of Morals and Legislation*. Oxford, Eng.: Basil Blackwell.

Blatz, Charles. 1972. "Accountability and Answerability." *Journal for the Theory of Social Behavior*. Vol. 2, No. 2, 101–120.

Boissonade, Prosper. 1982 (1964). *Life and Work in Medieval Europe*. Westport, Conn.: Greenwood.

Calabresi, Guido. 1970. *The Costs of Accidents*. New Haven, Conn.: Yale University Press.

Devlin, Patrick. 1965. *The Enforcement of Morals*. London: Oxford University Press.

Dostoyevsky, Fyodor. 1866 (1961). *Crime and Punishment*. Baltimore: Penguin Books.

Durham v. United States, 214, F. 2d 862 (1954).

Dworkin, Ronald. 1986. *Law's Empire*. Cambridge, Mass.: Harvard University Press.

Feinberg, Joel. 1970. *Doing and Deserving*. Princeton, N.J.: Princeton University Press.

———. 1985. *Offense to Others*. New York and Oxford, Eng.: Oxford University Press.

Feinberg, Joel and Hyman Gross, eds. 1986. *Philosophy of Law*, 3d ed. Belmont, Calif.: Wadsworth.

Flemming v. Nestor (80 S. Ct. 1367 [1960]).

French, Peter A., ed. 1972. *Individual and Collective Responsibility*. Cambridge, Mass.: Schenkman.

Fried, Charles. 1978. *Right and Wrong*. Cambridge, Mass.: Harvard University Press.

Fustel de Coulanges, Numa Denis. 1864. *The Ancient City*. New York: Doubleday.

Gagarin, Michael. 1986. *Early Greek Law*. Berkeley: University of California Press.

Gert, Bernard. 1966. *The Moral Rules*. New York: Harper & Row.

Golding, Martin P., ed. 1966. *The Nature of Law*. New York: Random House.

Gottfredson, Michael and Travis Hirschi. 1990. *A General Theory of Crime*. Stanford, Calif.: Stanford University Press.

Greenawalt, Kent. 1987. *Conflicts of Law and Morality*. New York: Oxford University Press.

Gutmann, Amy. 1987. *Democratic Education*. Princeton, N.J.: Princeton University Press.

Hall, Jerome. 1947. *General Principles of Criminal Law*, 2d ed. Indianapolis: Bobbs-Merrill.

Hammurabi. 1904 (about 2250 B.C.). *The Code of Hammurabi*, 2d ed. Translated by Robert F. Harper. Chicago: University of Chicago Press.

Hart, H. L. A. 1961. *The Concept of Law*. Oxford, Eng.: Clarendon Press.

———. 1966. *Law, Liberty, and Morality*. New York: Vintage Books.

———. 1968. *Punishment and Responsibility*. Oxford, Eng.: Oxford University Press.

———. 1983. *Essays in Jurisprudence and Philosophy*. Oxford, Eng.: Clarendon Press.

Herskovits, Melville J. 1950. *Man and His Works*. New York: Knopf.

Hobbes, Thomas. n.d. (1651). *Leviathan*. Oxford, Eng.: Basil Blackwell.

Hume, David. 1957 (1752). *An Inquiry Concerning the Principles of Morals*. New York: Liberal Arts Press.

Kant, Immanuel. 1965 (1797). *The Metaphysical Elements of Justice*. Translated by John Ladd. Indianapolis: Library of Liberal Arts.

———. 1785. *Groundwork of the Metaphysics of Morals*. (Many translations.)

Karpman, Benjamin. 1939. "Criminality, Insanity and the Law." *Journal of Criminal Law and Criminology*, p. 584.

Kleinig, John. 1973. *Punishment and Desert*. The Hague: Martinus Nijhoff.

Mill, John Stuart. 1956 (1857). *On Liberty*. Indianapolis: Bobbs-Merrill.

Model Penal Code. 1962. Philadelphia: The American Law Institute.

Morris, Herbert, ed. 1961. *Freedom and Responsibility*. Stanford, Calif.: Stanford University Press.

Nagel, Thomas. 1979. *Mortal Questions*. Cambridge, Mass.: Harvard University Press.

Newman, Graeme. 1978. *The Punishment Response*. Philadelphia: Lippincott.

Nietzsche, Friedrich. 1954 (1886). *Beyond Good and Evil*. In *Basic Writings of Nietzsche*. New York: Modern Library.

Owen, Robert. 1972 (1816). *A New View of Society: Or Essays on the Formation of the Human Character*, 2d ed. Clifton, N.J.: Augustus M. Kelley.

———. 1970 (1842). *The Book of the New Moral World*. New York: Augustus M. Kelley.

Paley, William. (1788). *The Principles of Moral and Political Philosophy*. (Many editions.)

Pincoffs, Edmund L. 1986. *Quandary Ethics: Against Reductivism in Ethics*. Lawrence: University Press of Kansas.

Radzinowicz, Leon. 1948. *A History of English Criminal Law and Its Administration from 1750*. London: Stevens and Sons.

Rawls, John. 1955. "Two Concepts of Rules." *Philosophical Review*, Vol. 64, No. 1, pp. 3–32.

———. 1971. *A Theory of Justice*. Cambridge, Mass.: Harvard University Press.

Royal Commission Report on Capital Punishment, 1949–53. 1953. London: Her Majesty's Stationery Office.

The Rules in M'Naghten's Case. 1843. 10 Cl. and F. 200 at p. 209.

Skinner, B. F. 1971. *Beyond Freedom and Dignity.* New York: Knopf.

Stephen, James Fitzjames. n.d. (1883). *A History of the Criminal Law of England.* New York: Burt Franklin.

Tolstoy, Leo. 1928 (1899). *Resurrection.* Translated by Louise Maude. London: Oxford University Press.

Wilson, Conlin. 1972. *The Mountain People.* N.Y.: Simon and Schuster.

Wilson, Edward O. 1975. *Sociobiology: The New Synthesis.* Cambridge, Mass.: Harvard University Press.

Wootton, Barbara. 1963. *Crime and the Criminal Law.* London: Sweet and Maxwell.

Zilboorg, Gregory. 1954. *The Psychology of the Criminal Act and Punishment.* New York: Harcourt, Brace.

Index

Abbott, Jack, 12
Acts, 4, 38, 53
  of conscientious violation of law, 126–129
  consequences of, 65–66
  defending and sentencing, 114–118
  differences between moral and legal,
    113–116
  mala in se, 131–132
  responsibility for legal, 64–65
Actus reus, 53, 73
Act utilitarians, 21
American Law Institutes's Model Penal
  Code, 72
Appraisals of desert, 30–31
Arbitrary liability, 63–64
Ascription of responsibility. *See*
  Responsibility-ascription practices
Assault, 131–132
Assignments of liability, 63–64
Atimia, 11–12
Austin, John, 92, 93, 94–95, 97, 107
Automobile no-fault insurance, 85–87

Benedict, Ruth, 50
Bentham, Jeremy
  on economy of threats, 73, 74

on natural law, 97, 129
  utilitarian beliefs of, 15, 19, 22, 124,
    134
Blame Responsibility, 56, 58
Boissonade, Prosper, 120–121

Calley, William L., 57
Capacity responsibility, 61
Capital punishment, 12, 41
Cardinal scale of punishment, 29
Categorical Imperative, 79
Causal responsibility, 61–62
Character
  education for, 139–140
  legal assessment of, 116–117
  morality of, 112–113
  virtue ethics and, 113–114
Code of Hammurabi, 73, 115
Comeuppances, 25
Compensation Responsibility, 56, 58
  arbitrary allocations and, 80–82
  laisser-tomber and, 79–80
  morality of, 77–78, 88
  no-fault insurances and, 82–87
Conscientious violation of law, 126–129
Consequences of acts, 103, 65–66

146

Hobbes, Thomas, 124, 135
Holmes, Oliver Wendell, Jr., 93, 100, 107
Homosexual behavior, law on, 5, 132–133, 134
Hugo, Victor, 24
Hume, David, 123–124

Immunity, 67–68, 73
Imprisonment, 5, 12, 39–41, 92
Incapacity defense, 67, 68–69, 73
Indifference Criterion, 79
Infant punishment, 15, 16, 74
Insanity defense, 4, 69
  M'Naghten Rules for, 69–72
Insurance. *See* No-fault insurance
Integrity
Irresistible impulse rule, 71

Jesus, 55
Justice
  in egalitarian systems, 120–122
  moral criteria of, 122–125
  nonegalitarian considerations of, 125–126
Justification, 67, 68, 73
Justification of punishment, 2, 5. *See also* Punishment
  capital, 41
  fairness of, 33–35
  fines as, 41–43
  imprisonment as, 39–41
  nature of, 22–23
  practices in, 37–39
  retributivist, 16–19, 25
  to society, 43–44
  system of rules in, 35–37

Kant, Immanuel
  on punishment, 16–17, 18, 19, 22, 24, 41
  on respect, 105
Karpman, Benjamin, 52

Laisser-tomber, 79–80, 81
Law
  assessment of character under, 116–117
  compensatory and no-fault liabilities under, 76–88
  conscientious violation of, 126–128
  criticisms of natural, 97–99
  defenses of liabilities under, 67–75

dilemmas of punishment by, 20–31
effect on moral education, 136–140
egalitarian systems of, 120–126, 130
on homosexual behavior, 132–133
justification of punishment by, 9–19, 33–34
mala in se, 131–132
morality in acts defended under, 114–116
natural theory of, 95–97, 101
positivist-realist theory of, 91–95, 100–101
as a practice, 2–3
reasonable man standard under, 133–134
relationship between moral rules and, 102–104, 109–110, 111–112, 113–114
responsibility-ascription practices of, 4–6, 58–66
rules and roles of, 3–4, 99–100
skepticisms of, 49–57
Legal positivism, 5, 91–93, 94–95
Legal punishment. *See* Punishment
Legal realism, 5, 93–95 Legal responsibility.
  See Responsibility-ascription practices
Les Misérables (Hugo), 24
Liability Responsibility
  assignments of, 63–64
  defined, 59–60, 61–62, 88
  individual and group, 62–63
  matching crime to, 28–30
  practices of, 60–61
  relationship of acts and harm to, 64–66
Lombroso, Cesare, 51
"Lord High Executioner" (Gilbert and Sullivan), 13

M'Naghten (Daniel) Rules, 69–71
  alternatives to, 71–72
Mala in se, 131–132
Mala prohibita, 131
Mens rea, 53, 54, 73
Metaphysical skepticism, 52–53
  and liability for an act, 65–66
Mill, John Stuart, 124, 138–139
Model Penal Code (American Law Institute), 72
Moral education programs, 5, 37, 136–140
Morality, 2, 5–6
  in arbitrary and group liability, 80–82
  of character, 112–114
  in Compensation Responsibility, 77–78, 88
  of conscientious violations of law, 126–128
  of Devlin, 134–136